ALSO BY JEFFERY SELF

*Drag Teen*

*A Very, Very Bad Thing*

# Self-Sabotage

*And Other Ways I've Spent My Time*

Jeffery Self

*An Imprint of* HarperCollins*Publishers*

HarperCollins books may be purchased for educational, business, or sales promotional use. For information, please email the Special Markets Department at SPsales@harpercollins.com.

FIRST EDITION

*Designed by Kyle O'Brien*

Library of Congress Cataloging-in-Publication Data has been applied for.

ISBN 978-0-06-332877-8

24 25 26 27 28 LBC 5 4 3 2 1

*To Augie, Cheech, and the boys of Dune House*

Everybody's got a sack of rocks.

—Elaine Stritch

# Contents

# Self-Sabotage

# Introduction

Hello and welcome to my book.

You there, yes you, that's a really lovely hat you're wearing.

Oh.

Really?

Are you sure?

Hmm. All right then, well, it's a really lovely hairdo.

There are a few reasons you may be holding this book.

First possible reason: you glued it to your hand on a dare. In which case, congrats, you won the dare, I guess? Cool? But also like . . . come on, you're an adult. Unless you're *not* an adult . . . in which case, I am going to politely ask you to put this book down right away.

Another possible reason: maybe you're holding this bad boy because . . . actually, let's not gender my book so quickly out of the gate.

This bad book.

Nope, strike that.

This book. By me. A boy. Some might even say a bad boy. Ugh, that's not it either.

I am a bad man.

Wait, no, sorry.

Let's just start over because we're really getting off on the wrong foot here.

Oh, I'm STANDING on your foot?! Jesus Christ. I'm so sorry!

Let's all just take a deep breath for a second.

Okay, we good? Good.

The next reason you might have picked up this book is that maybe you just liked the cover. That is totally valid, and I'm sure Jon Gray is as proud of it as I am, but I hope you'll continue actually reading it. Or at least / most important, buying it.

Another possible reason you picked up this book is the extremely unlikely chance you know who I am. I won't flatter myself and pretend that this minuscule group of people is anything more than a small cluster of like-minded degenerates who enjoy Christine Baranski and sucking dick as much as I do . . . but while we're on those two subjects, RIP, Stephen Sondheim. The ragtag band of folks who could have actually chosen this book on purpose may have seen me in something like my comedy sketches with the remarkable Cole Escola from 1,900 years ago or the TV show *Search Party*, which I was on for five seasons. Hmm? No, I was not the lead. Or even the second or third or fourth or fifth lead. Sixth? Why are we counting? I was on it, dammit!

When it comes to what has laughably been referred to as

my "career," things like no one remembering me from a show I was once on have gone from something that used to destroy my feelings to yet another thing I throw into the bed of my mental pickup truck: a beat-up, gas-guzzling hunk of rusted metal filled to the sky with my endless collection of tedious, time-wasting triggers.

I have squandered far too many of my previous years sinking into self-loathing despair when faced with a situation where something I acted in comes up and upon mentioning that I was in it am met with a blank stare. The person—let's say a gorgeous, curly-haired musical theater graduate from Carnegie Mellon in a still-damp-from-the-beach square-cut Speedo I've found myself trying to impress at middle tea on Fire Island, who has just claimed it's their "absolute number one favorite show of all time"—will look at me, his almond-colored eyes and box-cutter-sharp bone structure both dazzling yet slightly flawed like looking at Tom Holland through a keyhole, and say . . . "Um, no you weren't." In my darkest hours, ladies and gentlemen, I have argued my case, and never once has that not been followed by a wave of self-loathing.

Which brings me to the "self" in this book's title: perhaps yet one more reason you picked up this book. Maybe you saw the word "self" and thought this might be some form of self-help book where you could learn how to get out of your way own, to stop being your own worst enemy, to stop making choices you know on a gut level are the wrong ones, to forgive yourself.

And to those readers, I say, "Um, sort of, but also . . . not really."

I am a manic-depressive, and the pages you're about to read are probably best described as a word-based roller coaster through the chaos that is the unfortunate theme park of my mental health. Grab a funnel cake, but don't get too comfortable. I'm certainly not.

I have approached these stories from a place of self-reflection in an attempt to explore all the facets of my relationship with myself: self-loathing, self-employment, self-pity, self-harm, self-care, and of course . . . self-sabotage. You may notice I did not mention self-control, and that's because—spoiler alert!—I have none. Speaking of which, *Spoiler Alert* starring Jim Parsons and Sally Field is another of my film and TV credits. You literally just watched it on a plane last week? You don't remember me in it? I take Jim to the gay bar like five minutes into the movie in a pair of Lycra shorts in which you can see the outline of my flaccid penis if you pause it at the right moment before my character disappears for a solid forty minutes?

Ugh, fine, but we can all agree you are one of the sixty people who saw me on *The Horror of Dolores Roach*? My five-minute scene in *The High Note* with Dakota Johnson? The six minutes in *Mack and Rita* with Diane Keaton? My arc as a sassy gay hairdresser on *90210* in 2010?! I had those three lines and held that comb just so! Remember?!

Damn. This really isn't my day. But you know what? It IS my book.

In the following stories, you'll read about things like me losing my mind during my first breakup and documenting my every self-loathing-fueled move online until the authorities had to get involved. You'll read about me throwing literal shit out a window.

(Cleaning up after yourself—ever hear of it?) You'll read about me homeschooling myself online. You'll read about how, at just about every possible turn, I have found new and innovative ways of self-sabotage: chewing up and spitting out opportunities while making enemies out of friends and friends out of whoever hands me my Prozac prescription every month at Rite Aid.

There's a lot of that in this book—self-sabotage, I mean—certainly more than self-love or self-care, but who actually wants to read about my health routine? After all, there's only so much one can say about staring into the abyss and eating an entire box of Extra Toasty Cheez-Its while watching clips of Elizabeth Taylor talking about AIDS at 3:00 a.m. I think, for someone who grew up obsessively reading plays and watching movies, I'm always eager to flirt with the moment of the story where "all is lost," the part where the hero's pursuits are sabotaged in one way or another. I rush to this moment so that I can stop and rehearse what it will feel like, prepare myself for the moment when the shit hits the fan. Like on *I Love Lucy* when a very pregnant Lucy, along with Ricky, Ethel, and Fred, rehearse getting Lucy to the hospital for when she would eventually go into labor. I obsess so much over how terrible things *could be*, imagining the worst and eventually just giving in, giving up, deciding that's how it *is*, and sabotaging myself in the process. I try on all negative outcomes for size. I rip off the Band-Aid before I even scrape my knee. I guzzle the antidote and get too sick to ever try the poison. My actions tend to reflect that of a dress rehearsal for a play I have no real intention, and certainly am not prepared, to actually be in. I rehearse for the moment when all is lost because I always assume it inevitably will be. But it's time wasted because nothing ever goes as rehearsed. I mean, look at Lucy and Ricky. When the time came to get to the hospital to birth Little Ricky, did it go anywhere near as planned? No.

Hmm? Oh God, that's not what I mean! Of course the baby lived! Well, duh, yes Lucy lived too! She starred in four other TV series after that, left Desi, and single-handedly destroyed the movie version of *Mame*! I just mean, their rehearsing getting her to the hospital didn't make things any better. Certainly not the movie version of *Mame*.

My natural state seems to be standing at the edge of destruction but stopping right before I leap. Taking a path into the scary dark woods but leaving behind a trail of breadcrumbs so I can turn around and follow it back home when it gets *too* scary . . . like Hansel and Gretel heading off to that witch's house made of candy that is somehow not covered in ants.

Still, despite my flirtations with the dark, life continues to let sunlight through the cheap bamboo blinds of self-loathing that I've shoddily hung around all the windows to my self-indulgent heart, fearing that the golden rays of a lurking self-sufficiency will reveal all the grime and dust of self-pity so I can finally stop avoiding my habits of sabotage. I suppose this is an account of moments both joyful and not, to remind myself why it's not such a swell idea to someday self-sabotage for good and actually burn my life down to the crisp I so often fantasize will finally calm my mind. A life that often feels like a house made entirely of candy: cramped, sticky, a good and pretty idea in theory, sweet and colorful on the outside, but progressively rotting underneath.

Day to day I find myself striking a match and holding its

warmth in my hands, feeling the fire drift closer and closer to my fingertips as I stare at all I could sabotage. There, with the fiery power in my hand, I savor the idea of having nothing left to destroy. But at the last moment I stop and blow out the match, sparing the house, the candy, my world, and with it all . . . the ants.

# Ten Reasons Not to Sabotage Your Life

1. The first day of November when you notice Christmas decorations going up. But not when it's October, you freaks.
2. Getting to the 11th Street Cafe in the West Village while the raisin and pecan scones are still warm.
3. Marlene Dietrich's 1972 TV special.
4. Finding something so "you" at a flea market that you have to look around to make sure you shouldn't suddenly believe in God, like last summer when I woke up early enough to arrive at the Chelsea Flea Market the second it opened and immediately spotted a vintage locket necklace with a picture of Little Orphan Annie engraved onto it which had been released as official *Annie* movie merchandise in 1982. Gasping, I grabbed it with such ferocity that I knocked over everything else around it. The merchant took one look at me, and not

only did she understand my manic reaction . . . she also gave me a discount.

5. Sexy guys with armpits that are smelly but not *too* smelly.
6. Adding peanut butter to a spinach and kale smoothie.
7. The first sip of a Negroni just as the basket of garlic rolls arrives at your table, after you've ordered the chicken parm and a Caesar salad when having a solo dinner somewhere with a view of the street as you read Shelley Winters's second memoir titled simply *Shelley II.*
8. Wearing sunglasses and a hat in the airport and pretending to be famous.
9. The idea of going to the opera but not actually having to go.
10. Le Labo hand soap.

# Sweatin' to Sondheim

It wasn't until I met my friend Cole Escola that anyone in New York City gave a shit about what I was doing. We were introduced, like all great friendships between eighteen-year-old boys, by a fabulous fifty-something-year-old gay man / Broadway music arranger named Glen Kelly, who used to take us out to expensive dinners and show us Olivia de Havilland movies. Cole and I developed a pretty instant chemistry, and it was during one of these wine-soaked evenings that Glen suggested we make an exercise video sketch called "Sweatin' to Sondheim," wherein we'd show you how to exercise to the atonal music of the eminent Broadway composer.

It was 2007, and I had taken to YouTube as my main source of creativity by vlogging. My vlogs were made on a MacBook I somehow never paid for by purchasing through some sort of plan for students that Apple had at the time and then just, well, never paying. The vlogs were predictably narcissistic ramblings to the camera about my life or whatever I was obsessed with on TV, including a rant about one particularly hot contestant on *Project Runway*, which was seen by my dad's co-worker and ended up outing me to my parents as not just gay but gay and annoyingly attention-starved. Somehow they were genuinely surprised to discover both, but let's be honest, more so the former.

These vlogs were almost as indulgently audacious as someone writing an entire book of essays about himself. ALMOST. I wish I still had access to these video time capsules of my prospering ego, but at some point I manically deleted all of them because of, well, my ego. All of that is to say these videos weren't all that interesting, but as long as I got one hundred views, I could convince myself I was the next Johnny Carson.

Around this time I also started performing a show every Friday at midnight called *My Life on the Craigslist* at a theater in Hell's Kitchen that I rented with money made by my ongoing gig as a sex worker (more on that later). The title, of course, came from the popular Kathy Griffin show *My Life on the D-List*, and it was essentially a list of whatever online D I'd found that week, thanks to good old Craig. As my sole marketing tool, I went through Facebook and "friended" every gay man I could find in Manhattan before proceeding to harass each of them into attending. It actually sorta worked, and I slowly developed an extremely small following online and around the city.

But it wasn't until I added Cole to my videos that people really took notice—because while I was cute and funny, Cole was cute and REALLY, REALLY funny. We called ourselves the VGL Boys because "VGL" was a Craigslist personal ad term meaning "very good-looking." We figured that if people were searching for "VGL" on Craigslist, then maybe they'd do the same on YouTube and mistake us for porn. Which in some ways our videos were . . . if you had the incredibly specific kink of watching (now) nineteen-year-old boys make jokes about Joyce DeWitt in an apartment that was quite literally crumbling around them.

Cole started coming over every day around noon, which would usually end up being 1:00 p.m., and then we'd go to the bakery downstairs on Ninth Avenue, Amy's Bread, and spend money neither of us had on overpriced coffee and scones before spending a couple of hours gossiping, eventually getting around to an impressive twenty minutes of working around 4:00 p.m. Cole very quickly became my best friend, in that youthful way where neither of you ever mentions it but you both say yes to hanging out every day because neither of you has anything else going on and eventually you find yourselves finishing each other's sentences. It was a romance, complete with ups and downs, but with uproarious laughter replacing sexuality. Life was chaotic, very broke, scary, and aimless, but the minute Cole stepped into my orbit, I felt magic swirling around me at every moment and started to believe that things might actually work out someday.

Like every other gay guy who's written a book like this, I'd grown up making "movies" and forcing the kids in my neighborhood to be in them. Eventually the neighborhood kids stopped coming over entirely due to my demanding ways, and I begged my parents to buy me a dummy I'd seen in the JCPenney Christmas catalog a year or two prior. By the time my parents realized that this was not something that would disappear from my yearly Dear Santa list anytime soon, JCPenney had discontinued the dummy that they'd been selling. (I can't possibly imagine why.) True to supportive (bordering on enabling) form, my mother searched all over for an affordable replacement stunt dummy to give me an actor for my movies, by which we all knew but were afraid to admit meant a friend. Eventually they settled on what they didn't realize was essentially an inflatable sex dummy without genitals, and when I awoke that particular Christmas morning to find the human-size (completely nude with chest hair) inflated man that Santa had left standing over my other gifts, I screamed, "Oh my God! A costar!"

We named him Gomez because he looked a lot like Gomez Addams. He'd go on to star as a multitude of characters over the years. One day he'd be the dinner guest to my performance as a fussy waiter who had never heard of Cobb salad; the next he'd be decked out in full grandma drag jumping out a window as I screamed for him off camera, "I am the Diarrhea Queen!"

Like all great creative partnerships, however, my inflatable dummy and I eventually parted ways—in this case because he had a hole puncturing his thigh and I could no longer inflate him. But ah, the films we made. John Cassavetes and Gena Rowlands are said to have gone through something eerily similar. Don't look that up. Just trust me.

So then, all those years later, I met Cole, and while I could say a lot about Cole, they are as far as it gets from a dummy OR inflatable. Hell, I'm not sure they can even swim. And all those days of wanting to turn on my camcorder and make myself laugh but having no one to play with were over.

In the early days of our friendship, I was pretty nervous around Cole. My usual need to impress was hard to fulfill while simultaneously revealing my shitty apartment, despite the fact that Cole's apartment was so shitty I never even saw it. To get to the bathroom, I had to go through my constantly sleeping roommate's spooky bedroom or travel into the harsh fluorescent light of the building's hallway, so I had developed the pretty disgusting habit of peeing in empty jars and bottles in the middle of the night, then hiding them behind my bookshelf. By the time Cole and I were making videos in my bedroom, I had what could only be described as the Metropolitan Museum of My Urine, in various stages of mold, hidden behind my shelf of the Samuel French scripts I'd stolen from my hometown community theater. I was pretty lazy about cleaning up after myself, and one very late night when I ran out of empty bottles, I hastily dumped one out my window before hearing an unfortunate someone walking by scream in disgust. I was so afraid of being caught for my pee-pee dumping that I didn't leave my apartment for two days, as if a person would have waited forty-eight hours (covered in my moldy piss) to confront me for my sick twist on the long-forgotten "ice bucket challenge."

So, it was there in a bedroom full of my rapidly aging bottled urine that Cole and I began our comedy careers. People had liked the "Sweatin' to Sondheim" video enough that we were inspired to keep going. The internet had started heating up over gay marriage becoming legal in California, and it was impossible to read about anything else. It's my first memory of gay people on the internet banding together to celebrate a gay win, and my first thought was, *We gotta capitalize on this!* So, I AIM-ed Cole to say we needed to make a video about it immediately. Cole came over and we threw something together, posted it online, and did what we would end up doing a lot over the next few years: went out to celebrate our two hours of work by getting completely shit-faced.

We had just finished dinner at Yaffa Cafe in the East Village and were walking up St. Mark's when I got an email notification on my BlackBerry Curve saying our recent video had already reached five thousand views. It had only been up for a few hours, and these were MAJOR numbers for us. It was as if this had been 1998 and *Dharma and Greg* suddenly got *Friends* ratings. We rushed back to my apartment to find out how this had happened, flying high on our success. Bye-bye, Jenna Elfman. Hello, Jenna Aniston.

We discovered that the 2008 gay equivalent of Lana Turner being discovered at the soda fountain had happened: we were featured on *Perez Hilton* somewhere between a picture of Suri Cruise's new shoes and an unflattering paparazzi photo of Nicole Richie with a hastily drawn sketch of a penis over her mouth. The video comments started piling up, Facebook friend requests from hot guys in LA started coming through, and we knew that the only logical next step was to perform a two-person show in the city and become internationally beloved superstars.

We got to work on a show, with the help of two of our closest friends: the actor Christian Coulson and the director Michael Arden (who would eventually go on to win a Tony Award . . . NOT for our show). Taking a page out of our "VGL Boys" link to internet sex lingo, we called the show *Party and Play*, or *PnP*, which was, and often still is, how guys denote in personal ads their desire to do crystal meth and have sex. I'd recently learned the term the hard way when the number one bartender at a nearby bar called Posh invited me over from Adam4Adam.com at 3:00 a.m. on a Monday to hook up. When I got there, both his TV and laptop were playing dueling videos of hard-core porn, and he offered me a pipe that I figured was weed before realizing it actually wasn't (just in the nick of time). But yes, I stayed for half an hour, before eventually climaxing and never darkening the halls of Posh again.

We came up with the title before the show, then wrote the show to encapsulate it—the way they did with *Hamilton* or *Bad Cinderella*. We decided the premise of the show was that we were in my apartment putting on a show, but all the while Cole was annoyed because I'd forgotten their birthday, and in the final act we had to throw a party together. Think Ibsen, then . . . don't.

Proposition 8, the California proposition to ban gay marriage, was on the ballots in 2008, and once again the internet was heating up, and once again I suggested we capitalize on it. In the resulting video, we used the only thing gayer than gay marriage: Cole as Bernadette Peters. Cole had recently purchased an uncanny Bernadette wig and had perfected her arm movements from the *Bernadette Peters Live at Carnegie Hall* DVD, so it was simply a matter of arithmetic. Soon, riding on the success of that video, *Party and Play* ended with Bernadette Peters crashing the party and the audience going nuts for Cole's pitch-perfect performance.

We first performed the show in the basement of the Daryl Roth Theatre off Union Square. We charged five dollars a ticket, and somehow it ended up being standing room only. We were ecstatic until we realized the person we'd found on Facebook to collect cash at the door had stolen more than half the money while we were too busy drinking in our success (and white wine) to notice.

We then got invited to perform the show at Joe's Pub a few times. The show wasn't stand-up or sketch comedy per se, and it certainly was not a play—more of a fever dream sitcom. Think a less iconic *Laverne and Shirley* but on acid, then lower your expectations by half and do more acid. It's hard to recall exactly what happened in the show, but I do remember that after Bernadette Peters left the stage and Cole returned, Cole pulled out a gun and shot my foot so we couldn't do a "play" but could instead "party."

Having grown up as an egomaniac who was aggressively addicted to being the most unique person in the room, I found that my collaboration with Cole became trickier the more popular we became. Like all comedy duos, one of us was more of the straight man (me) and one of us was more of the wacky scene-stealer (Cole). I obviously knew Cole was unlike anyone else who'd ever existed, and while I also knew I was unique, I read the online comments beneath our videos like a drug. Social media and comment culture were new, but people had already more than discovered the beloved pastime of hating strangers who put themselves out there and made sure that the stranger knew how awful they were. Or in our case, how much funnier Cole was than me.

Let's be clear: NO ONE is more unique or funnier than Cole Escola, but I don't think my now barely twenty-year-old brain knew how to balance both being in awe of them and also how to be their creative partner without getting constantly derailed by jealousy. But did I ever bring this up or address it in any way other than internal shame and self-loathing? Of course not, silly goose! Push it down, pretend it's not real, drink that Trader Joe's two-buck wine, rinse, repeat. I didn't have time to think through my shit; we were too busy being on our little hodgepodge niche gay roll.

Soon enough we were contacted by a gay stranger on Facebook (is there any other kind?) who offered to fly us to LA, put us up (in his guest room overlooking Hollywood Boulevard), and film a "sizzle reel" for a "reality show." By which I mean, we were flown to LA to get drunk with this only slightly handsy gentleman, go around town with a cameraman following us, and do HILARIOUS stuff like get spray tans and help Bruce Vilanch down the stairs at a gay fundraiser at the Mondrian Hotel (harder than it looks!). Each day was more and more demoralizing, and on our last night in LA, Cole and I were sitting on the balcony overlooking a cinematic view of Hollywood, fighting back drunken tears as we pined to go home to New York, where people wanted more Bernadette Peters and less us using flip-cams to interview tweaked-out go-go dancers at the Abbey.

Once back in the safety of our awful New York apartments, we were back to performing *Party and Play*, making videos, and feeling like hot shit. That's when we were invited to perform on a gay cruise to the Caribbean by the same Facebook stranger who had brought us to LA. It was a bitterly cold January in New York, and it felt like the biggest of breaks to be hired to go perform on a boat full of gay guys for a week. Cole was immediately skeptical after our experience in LA, but I had the emerald waters of the

Caribbean in my freezing eyes. The problems started as soon as we remembered neither of us had passports and found out that being "hired" to perform on this boat meant we were merely being invited to stay for free while all the other performers were actually being paid. The Facebook stranger agreed to pay for our rushed passports, and as we waited outside an office near Penn Station to get them, Cole asked me if I was sure I wanted to do this, pointing out that neither of us had any money whatsoever to spend while on the boat. I retorted that the food would be free and that after we performed our first show, everyone on the boat would be obsessed with us and would buy us drinks all week.

This was always a key difference between Cole and myself: while I was desperate for anything that felt like success, Cole has always been capable of letting things grow naturally and becoming good at whatever pace it takes.

When I say our experience on that January 2009 weeklong gay cruise out of Miami was bad, it's like saying the icebergs *might* be melting. We boarded the boat, where the stranger from Facebook who'd gotten us booked plowed us with vodka Red Bulls a few hours before we were set to perform our show on the first night of the voyage. The vibe was immediately not quite what I'd call "us." Electronic dance music blared out of every possible corner of this floating gay metropolis, which was promoted as "the biggest gay cruise of all time," and the instantaneously Speedo-clad men (did they arrive that way from the Miami Airport?) were already grinding and fucking on every available surface of the ship in broad daylight.

The entertainment for that first evening was quite literally

Charo on the main stage followed by us in the medium-size cabaret room called the Pharaoh's Lounge, which you'd better believe was decorated in 100 percent problematically misused Egyptian decoration. We didn't have a "cruise act," but instead simply opted to perform the same *Party and Play* show we'd been performing to young and old New York show queens for the past few months. If it ain't broke, don't fix it . . . unless, we'd soon learn, you're bringing it on a boat.

Cole and I, buzzed on the vodka Red Bulls in the Miami sun, anxiously rehearsed our show before we went upstairs to watch Charo. Sure, we had a show to prepare for, but if you're on a cruise with Charo, you watch Charo. That's called being a human being. As we stood in the back of the enormous theater where the cruise director was welcoming the audience to Charo, any excitement or confidence we'd been feeling quickly dissipated.

"And after this, I've got a question for you," the gay cruise director said into his microphone, exactly how you'd imagine the director of a gay cruise with access to a microphone to speak. "Who likes to laugh?"

The thousand or so gay men in the sold-out theater all cheered uproariously.

"And who in here likes hot young TWINKS?!" the cruise director continued, which was obviously met with more cheering. "Well, then, head on up to the Pharaoh's Lounge after Charo for two of the funniest, hottest, bitchiest twinks you'll ever meet: Jeffery and Cole!"

The crowd cheered as Cole and I melted into the back wall of the theater. I swallowed a lump in my throat the size of the lifeboat I suddenly wanted to escape in as any hope that this would be the magical week I'd insisted it would be faded from my mind like the mainland had just done as we set sail into the middle of the Atlantic. We had two hours until showtime (which ended up being three because, well, Charo), and there was no turning back now.

As we stood behind the curtain waiting to go on, it seemed as if every drunk gay man from Charo's electrifyingly successful show had crammed into the Pharaoh's Lounge. We'd done the show a dozen times in New York at that point, so we knew the show like the back of our hands. The only problem was that this fired-up crowd would've preferred hand jobs to our comedy. While there was no argument we were twinks, and I'd venture to say even funny, we weren't all that bitchy, and we weren't necessarily the type this crowd would find "hot." Within two minutes of the start of our show, the crowd had turned against us. They were too drunk, we were too drunk, and the show was completely wrong for this floating venue on the sea. Where they wanted dick jokes and Lady Gaga references, we offered asides about poopy enema water and Shelley Long. We were bombing before the clock had hit ten minutes, and by bomb I don't mean the 1996 Olympic Village—I'm talking Pearl Harbor. People booed, literally threw things at the stage, and finally walked out until only five people who had taken pity on us remained. We were both covered in sweat and communicating complete and utter failure into each other's eyes by the time the show approached its merciless end. When even Cole as Bernadette Peters didn't fix anything, I knew the goose was cooked. In the show's final moments, Cole returned to the stage to shoot my foot in the big finale, but as they reached for their pocket, they realized they'd forgotten to pack the gun entirely. So instead, they took a fork off a now hauntingly empty table in the front row, saying with little to no energy whatsoever: "I'm going to stab your foot with this fork." Then we turned to the audience mid-scene and bowed dejectedly, leaving the stage to what can't even be considered scattered applause. It was more like the sound of an old southern grandma clapping her hands together to shoo away a stray dog: "Get! Go on now!"

We stood behind the curtain, completely destroyed, until the tech person came back to get our microphones and assure us that everyone had left. It was pretty clear that absolutely no one on the boat was going to be obsessed with us, and certainly nobody would be buying us drinks.

We retreated to our windowless staterooms with our heads down like two fugitives on the run before locking ourselves inside. We sat together for a bit, both emotional wrecks, fighting back tears not unlike the ones we'd shed on that Hollywood balcony, once again wishing more than anything to be back in New York. I didn't leave my room for the next twenty-four hours. Instead I downed the single free bottle of red wine that had come with the room and popped three Tylenol PM, savoring each drop of the shitty wine going down my throat, knowing I wouldn't be able to buy more.

A full day later, as the boat made its way somewhere toward Haiti, Cole knocked on my door, awaking me from my slumber/coma.

"I went up to the buffet and saw Alec Mapa and Miss Richfield

1981. They said that nobody is mad at us. Do you want to come get some food?"

I agreed.

In a cap and sunglasses like a recently canceled Bravolebrity, I followed Cole up to the buffet, where we spent the rest of the day eating our feelings. The dessert buffet almost made up for the cruise's complete lack of any fun whatsoever. Unless, of course, I happened to glance around the room and spot the countless clusters of gay men staring at us and whispering to each other. We were certainly celebrities on the boat, but not for the reason I'd hoped. When stuck in an elevator with someone and accidentally making eye contact, the person would usually say something along the lines of "We saw your show the other night" in the sympathetic tone you'd use when speaking to a 9/11 widow.

Luckily, there was one glimmer of hope. I arrived back to my stateroom to find that Ben Rimalower, a dear friend of mine and Cole's, had figured out a way to wire us three hundred dollars. Ben knew we were boarding the boat penniless, and whether he'd received a Mayday from a gay he knew on board who had seen our first night's comedic disaster or if he had some sort of witchy sense that things hadn't gone as planned, I don't know. He did whatever the hell he had to do to get us the cash we'd need to survive the next few days, not to mention the cab from the boat to the plane once we got back to the mainland. That is, IF we got back to the mainland alive.

The sword of Damocles still hung over our hungover heads because we still had to do the show AGAIN later in the week, having been strongly encouraged by the person who'd booked us to come up with something (absolutely anything) else to perform. We had been demoted to the small piano bar, and the boat promoted us with the enthusiasm you'd use to promote a broken toilet at a chili cook-off on the hottest day of August in Shreveport, Louisiana. As the boat approached Puerto Rico, I hastily downloaded as many karaoke tracks as I could in the ten minutes of internet my debit card could pay for, with the idea that Cole singing "Whatever Lola Wants" could obtain forgiveness for our sins.

The night of the show, Cole threw on a mermaid costume they'd brought along at the last minute and sang to a scattershot selection of karaoke tracks, I told some sex stories from my old *My Life on the Craigslist* show, and we both made as many references as possible to our tightly pristine buttholes and told the type of "isn't this hilarious because we're all on the same boat and gay"–type jokes they wanted—like "Lido deck? More like libido deck. Right, boys?" All in all, the twelve people who attended (or happened to already be drunk in that particular bar and couldn't be bothered to move) enjoyed the show enough for me not to spend another twenty-four hours locked in my stateroom.

The trip did end on a high note, however, when the cruise's "surprise guest performer" was revealed to be none other than Patti LuPone, fresh off her run in *Gypsy* on Broadway. As soon as we heard that she was somewhere on the boat, our morning turned into playing a live-action variation of *Where's Waldo?* It wasn't long before we found ourselves face-to-face with Mama Rose herself as she stepped into a crowded elevator with a plate of scrambled egg whites she'd just gotten from the breakfast buffet.

One queen behind us called out, "Patti, that's all you're eating?" And she replied, "I'm feeling seasick, doll." Another queen eagerly chimed in, "I'm sure someone can get you Dramamine," and without skipping a beat, Patti joked, "I want quaaludes!" The elevator door slammed in front of her, right on cue.

She performed two standing-room-only shows on the final night. Cole and I sat in the front row, refusing to move between performances in fear of losing our seats, again tearfully holding on to each other, not unlike that first awful night in our staterooms following our terrible show. But this time the tears were for joy, the type of joy you can only feel when you're a twenty-one-year-old, stuck aboard a boat somewhere in the Caribbean full of gay guys who booed you, watching Patti LuPone sing "English Teacher" from *Bye Bye Birdie*, having just overdrawn your checking account to buy a karaoke track of "Whatever Lola Wants."

Cole and I returned to New York with a newfound dose of humility beneath the tails stuck between our legs and went back to performing together for like-minded audiences around town while also making our silly videos. Around that same time, some folks at Logo, the Viacom-owned gay TV network, reached out to us through Facebook to set up a meeting, and suddenly things felt that much more exciting. Two very nice gay executives took us out to a fancily boozy dinner and offered us a "development deal" that included the obligation for us to make a series of twenty-two-minute vlogs that the network would have permission to put on television if they so chose.

Without reps or anyone to advise us otherwise, we eagerly signed the deal for five thousand dollars to be split between the two of us. I was rich, or I felt like I was until after I'd cashed the check at a twenty-four-hour check-cashing place behind Port Authority and spent it all on roughly four trips to Bar Centrale, the ultra-fancy cocktail lounge above Joe Allen's that's so exclusive they don't even have a sign. Cole and I had started going there with our friend Lisa Lambert, who had won a Tony for writing *The Drowsy Chaperone*. Lisa brought us there so often that the snooty maître d' (let's call her Mary because that's her actual name and she still works there) was guilted into letting us sit at the bar when we'd show up before all the Broadway shows let out, at which time we'd be booted off our stools for people who could actually afford to be there and who might even order food. Eventually, Nathan Lane discovered our videos and brought us there one particularly joyous night after gifting us tickets to see him brilliantly perform in the less-than-brilliant Broadway adaptation of *The Addams Family*. It was impossible not to feel on top of the world being greeted by an all-time idol such as Nathan fucking Lane, and to make matters better, the look on Mary's face when we waltzed into Bar Centrale behind the king of Broadway himself was not dissimilar to when Miss Hannigan finds out Daddy Warbucks is adopting Annie. NYC, indeed.

When I had heard about Logo's "development deal," I imagined a Jeffery and Cole sitcom or even a made-for-TV movie, but all they really wanted was for us to make those twenty-two-minute vlogs, aka a full-blown sketch show made from my apartment, starring, written by, directed by, edited by, and produced by us. They provided us with zero budget but gave us full control, making it the type of nightmare that was the greatest thing that had ever happened to me.

We spent every day writing our stupid sketches, then making them on that same busted laptop I never paid for in my apartment where, yes, I was still pissing in bottles. We played all the parts with the exception of sometimes getting a friend to join in the chaos in exchange for our appreciation and a sandwich from the bakery downstairs. Luckily our friends were geniuses at the beginning of their own careers—friends like Bridget Everett, Erin Markey, Max Steele, Michael Cyril Creighton, Rachel Shukert, Joseph Keckler, Christian Coulson, Lisa Lambert, Taylor Trensch, Blake Daniel, Harriet Holloway, the great Justin Vivian Bond, and Eric Gilliland, who was actually more successful than anyone I knew but had made so much nineties sitcom money that he was bored enough to say yes.

Every few weeks, we'd upload the latest episode to a bulky hard drive Logo provided us, then we'd lug it over to their offices in Times Square to drop it off and steal snacks from their break room. A few months into this highly professional enterprise, they informed us they'd be putting the "show" on "TV" every Friday night at midnight following an all-day *Buffy the Vampire Slayer* marathon.

That summer the show premiered, and we also performed a monthlong run of a new live show called *Jeffery and Cole Make It Bigger* at Dixon Place in the Lower East Side. Things couldn't have been going better . . . unless of course we had actually been getting paid. From the success of the show, we ended up with a manager who started submitting us for auditions, and it wasn't long before all my insecurities about Cole's talent and overall specialness exceeding my own took on the same volume as the trucks and sirens blaring past my Midtown window every night. Cole quickly booked a one-off guest role on *Law and Order*, and I was as triggered as I'd have been had they won an Academy Award. My nasty habit of comparing myself to my genius friend was getting more and more out of control, the online comments from cruelhearted strangers serving as gasoline upon the fire I'd started myself, but even though I knew the flames were damaging to my eyes and heart, it was impossible to look away. Each day my plate of jealousy grew with resentment, slowly but surely, until it was an entire feast.

Around the same time, Logo asked us to make more episodes of the show, even giving us a new deal with slightly more than no money and teaming us up with a production company that was also producing Sherri Shepherd's short-lived and self-titled Lifetime sitcom, from which they gave us the wigs they didn't use. Free wigs? A tenuous, at best, connection to a cohost of *The View*? Everything was coming up . . . if not roses, then something rose-adjacent, and it felt good.

With our new producers, we were able to make requests. We'd say, "We really need a clown nose, a tripod, and ten pounds of raw ground beef to rub all over our bodies"—and we got it! The network continued to be mostly hands-off, giving us a creative playground to screw around in. They only put their feet down when we submitted a script that included Jessica Lange admitting to murdering a kindergarten class.

Eventually, our creative partnership began to lose steam and inspiration for a multitude of reasons. It was a lot of work for two incredibly inexperienced people who'd only been legally eligible to vote in one presidential election at that point. Atop our immaturity, I was by then out of control with comparing myself to Cole at every turn. I had gotten myself to the point that I was incapable of ever enjoying anything we did together, always aware of the nagging inner voice convinced the audience just wanted me to go away. Even now, as I write that very sentence, I imagine you reading it and thinking, *Yep! Correct!* And maybe a lot of people did, but I also (now) know we were doing good stuff and all that my own self-loathing did for our work was make me retreat further into the claustrophobic closet of my head and hate myself that much more.

Our collaboration never "ended" but instead fizzled out slowly and without the type of grand finale that might have offered some cathartic closure. In August 2010, I moved to LA in what was supposed to be a visit but became thirteen years. As our paths diverged, we continued growing up but without the daily connection we'd once had. I suppose that's how long-lasting friendships always work, but until Cole, I'd never known what a friendship like that was. With Cole, I'd found a kid like me after an entire childhood of being convinced that such a person did not exist.

As time went on, Cole continued doing their thing, experiencing their own very bumpy journey, which they can tell about in their own book. However, Cole slowly figured out their lane, becoming more and more successful as they evolved into the brilliant artist they are today. Meanwhile, upon going to LA and never coming back, I committed myself to getting further and further away from the sense of humor Cole and I had shared. I was afraid to try anything remotely close to the sort without Cole because I was deeply convinced no one wanted it from me. Instead, I ran toward being "basic" because if I did that, at least I'd never have to compete with someone as special as my former comedy partner again. I threw myself into hosting gigs. I did movie review videos for Logo's website with my then-boyfriend where the hook was that we were shirtless and one of us had abs (it wasn't me). I hosted things like "Fan Cam Live Presented by Trident Gum" backstage at the MTV Movie Awards, where I stood in a tight electric blue suit from Zara, earning my appearance fee by keeping a straight face while I pretended to know what the fuck the words "Camila Cabello" meant. I appeared on recap shows about *The Bachelor* covered in pancake makeup and regret. I hosted "digital content," like a Snapchat series produced by E! about Kardashian conspiracy theories. With a lot of denial and weed smoking, I was able to almost convince myself that I was happy while squinting my eyes to read a teleprompter's regrettable lines about just how much fiercer Khloé was than Kim—or maybe it was the other way around. I still don't fucking care. I sprinted as far away from the type of things that used to make Cole and me laugh, and by doing so, I ran far, far, far away from myself.

There were little bursts of light in those years where Cole and I would end up back together. We performed a live show in NYC called *Postcards from the Edge, Part Two: Edith Head's Revenge*; we were brought to Australia to perform at Sydney Mardi Gras; and we had small parts in a made-for-MTV movie filmed in

New Orleans called *Ladies Man* that absolutely no one saw and that luckily seems to have been buried beneath the earth's core or at least in Viacom's vault. But it would never be the same as it had been in those trying times of our early days. Perhaps the magic had simply faded, or perhaps my insecure comparison of myself to my brilliant friend had finally gotten so far out of control that there was no turning back. The more Cole did, the more they continued to soar into their authentic self, the more I retreated.

At some point a few years ago, something changed. Probably a combination of many things: growing up, therapy, being married, too long in LA, time in general. Whatever it was, I finally wrote something new for the two of us to do again. It was called *Bunny and Clyde*. While I was very proud of this script, I couldn't bring myself to show Cole. The thing I always saw as the inevitable had happened: Cole's career had, in fact, become much better without me. I was convinced they'd have to turn me down, and if that happened, I worried it would officially destroy whatever frayed strands of motivation I had left. So I tried to do the show with someone else, but that ended up not working out, and at the very last minute I showed it to Cole in fear of losing the producers who were behind it. Cole immediately agreed, and soon enough they flew to LA and we filmed a "pilot presentation" as a sales tool.

We spent two very long days filming together for the first time in nearly a decade. It was almost as ragtag and thrown together as it had been back in my Hell's Kitchen apartment, except with an actual director (the great Bridey Elliott) along with real cameras and sound. From the start, it was as if all those years of my horrid Snapchat hosting and shirtless movie reviewing never happened and I was still talking into my old busted MacBook with my old dear genius friend. That pilot presentation got bought by HBO Max but died along with the streaming network itself in the type of corporate merger that always seems to happen the minute you get let into the corporation.

But the gift of that experience was that it reminded me to have gratitude when looking back at those years of collaborating with one of the most talented people I've ever met. It all happened at such a young age, one that seems to have passed as quickly now as it felt slow and arduous at the time. I was too immature and naive to realize just how lucky we were to be hustling through such a scrappily creative and special time together. Now, almost two decades later—with a rearview mirror looking back at that awful gay cruise, that terrible afternoon of Hollywood spray tans, the day we covered ourselves in raw ground beef in front of an inexpensive camcorder in the blazing summer sun on my Hell's Kitchen roof, the numerous shows and videos where I spent most of my brainpower comparing myself to my genius collaborator instead of appreciating the ride—I see just how lucky I was.

It can feel odd to have planted the seedlings of one's career in a "duo." As you grow and shift in different directions, it can be discombobulating to inevitably continue comparing yourself to what was once your other creative half, just as you did all those years before. But within those growing pains, I see just how cool it is that any of it ever happened at all.

Still, when I find myself in a room with Cole again—writing or just hanging out or leaping to my feet to join in the standing ovation at their Broadway triumph, *Oh, Mary!*—I am reminded of how special it is that our eighteen-year-old selves found each other in the chaos of New York City. Whenever I find myself engaged in the type of creativity that makes me forget what day or time it is, it is those early years with Cole that I am reminded of: days inside my shitty apartment above a bakery, broke and too ambitious for our own good, jars of my molding piss hidden behind a bookshelf of Samuel French scripts, with my busted laptop filming us as we made each other laugh like a kid with an inflatable dummy in place of friends (but now, finally, with a real friend who just happens to be the funniest person who ever lived) while we were sweatin', sweatin' to Sondheim . . . and on my most uninspired of days, I long to hit PAUSE and stay there forever.

# Golden Son

*The wheels on the bus go round and round,*
*round and round,*
*round and round.*
*Sarah Ann on the bus goes wahhh wahhh wahhh,*
*wahhh wahhh wahhh,*
*wahhh wahhh wahhh.*

Those "wahhhs" are meant to be the sound of an annoyingly shrill baby crying, and this ditty is what my Dad and I used to sing to my older sister anytime we were in the car together, just for the mere pleasure of hurting her feelings. And ah, how we laughed.

My sister is five years older than me. She's the middle child between my older half brother and myself: the very spoiled, very coddled, and still very needy youngest, the baby. Wahhh wahhh wahhh.

My sister was a tough kid, and nowadays she's the toughest adult I know. She works with very young students at a Georgia public school, where she is paid maddeningly little for the enormous heart she brings to her job. She gets up early every morning to wrangle a room full of screaming five-year-olds by 7:00 a.m. She's overcome rough periods that could have done most people in—but she navigated them, all on her own.

Not too long ago, she came home from work and discovered a random tweaked-out man standing in the middle of her kitchen. Upon seeing this stranger, she stopped dead in her tracks, and screamed, "What the fuck are you doing in my house?!"

The meth madman had the audacity to look directly at her and in a condescendingly calm tone falsely advised, "Ma'am, I'm not in your house."

Without breaking eye contact, this literal thief then turned, opened the refrigerator, and gingerly took out an opened can of Diet Dr Pepper that he'd apparently stored there while ransacking my sister's home. As the man brought it to his lips, my sister charged at him, screaming even louder this time, "Get the fuck out of my house!"

She chased him into the street while calling 911. When I asked her if, during this insane moment, she was scared, she took a sip from her can of Coors Light and shrugged, replying with the baddest-ass suave, "Eh. Mostly I just wanted him to, well, get the fuck out of my house."

My sister was born tough, but I sometimes wonder if my relentlessly vampiric need to suck up all the attention and make everything about me forced her to toughen up even more. Not unlike how I just made her toughness all about me in this very book. Throughout childhood, I created a dynamic of getting my parents to unite with me in making my sister a punch line for the sake of my own comedic routine / our daily lives because it was the easiest way to get the laugh and deflect from every part of myself that I was born knowing to be ashamed of.

"The Wheels on the Bus" was one of many pieces in my repertoire of the musical bullying I put her through. Another was a solid three-to-ten-year period of loudly humming the witch's theme from *The Wizard of Oz* anytime she came into a room. And again, ah, how we all laughed.

When she and a neighbor wouldn't let me join them in playing Nintendo, I went outside, gathered up an enormous pile of dog shit with a stick and a paper plate I'd pilfered from the garbage, then covered her bike and the neighbor's bike in it. The neighbor's parents were rightfully furious, but mine? Ah, how we laughed.

We all know that parents of multiple children are often far more lax with their youngest out of sheer exhaustion, and while I think that definitely played a part in the dynamic I forced my mom and dad into, what it really boiled down to was that I was better at playing the role of the golden child while my sister was just, well, a real person. For better or worse, she was a real kid, while I always felt like a calculated huckster pretending to be one. I was desperate to be liked by my already loving parents, obsessed with making them accept me before they ever showed any indication they wouldn't. Most stories I'd heard regarding people who came out as gay to their southern parents involved a narrative of nonacceptance. I was stocking up love like canned goods before getting hit by the inevitable earthquake of finding out I was unlovable.

As my sister grew older, she leaned more and more into rebellion, while I leaned more and more into convincing my parents I wasn't gay and crazy but, rather, special and bound for success. I suppose I'm still attempting to convince myself and anyone I encounter the very same thing. I continued to get away with pretty much anything I wanted. Don't want to go to high school? Response to my sister: "Shut up and get to school." Response to me: "Oh fine, you can homeschool yourself and go to yoga classes with your mom and other older women twice a week for your credit in PE."

What had been a sweet and sometimes competitive little brother / big sister dynamic when we were kids devolved to outright resentment as we grew up. For her, it was how spoiled I was, and for me, it was that I saw my sister's rebellion as a thing that would destroy our family. She was a nineties teenager with Kurt Cobain posters, platform Dr. Martens, and a rapidly progressing substance problem that everyone seemed to be pretending didn't exist. I missed the big sister of our early childhood years, the sister who would do dress rehearsals for Christmas morning with me in the middle of the summer and who wanted to play Young Cosette in a national tour of *Les Misérables* almost as much as I did.

By the time she graduated from high school, she was rarely around. When she was, our house turned into an amateur production of *August: Osage County*. My parents didn't know how to handle her. No one seemed to be in charge, but everyone seemed to be furious. I'd always join my parents in bitching about my sister—always taking their side over hers, even when I knew she wasn't in the wrong because that's what golden children do.

When my grandfather died, it had been a while since any of us had seen my sister. She showed up for my mom and reentered our lives for that strange week that follows a death, when all the cousins come together like it's a holiday. Instead of presents, though, you're all just stealing your parents' Xanax and trying not to cry as you mourn yet another step away from the already vanishing childhoods you all shared.

After the funeral, my sister and I ended up driving back from the cemetery to the church to pig out on fried chicken and casseroles (because who isn't hungry after burying somebody?). It was the first time we'd been alone, just the two of us, in a very long time. My parents were still obsessed with their golden child even as I grew into the progressively gayer and crazier person I am today, they were still celebratiiing my every move and letting me do whatever the fuck I wanted. Meanwhile, my sister's life was an isolated, chaotic mess that I never missed the chance to join my parents in judging her for.

But as we pulled into the church parking lot, there were no parents to impress. There was just us, a pipe, and a big bag of weed.

"I need to smoke before we go in there," she said. "Want some?"

At this point, I had never tried weed or drunk more than a sip or two of my dad's beer. Seeing as I'd always leaned on my sister's bad habits as a way of convincing my parents that I was the good one and that they had absolutely nothing to worry about when it came to me (GAY! GAY! GAY!), my instinct was to say no thanks.

But I also knew that trying weed for the first time with my estranged sister in a church parking lot after my grandfather's funeral would be a good story to include in a book someday. So, there we were, and here we are.

We got high and did all the things you do when you first get high, coughing and laughing and having the type of heart-to-heart that feels profound but is ultimately just hard to remember at all.

"I have to tell you something," I said between tokes, "I'm gay."

"Well, duh," she said. "Do you know how many fucking people I've had to beat up over the years for calling you a fag?"

I'd never really thought about it until that moment, but my sister *had* always been my protector, my bodyguard, the toughest person I knew. Somewhere along the way I'd stopped seeing her as my protector but as the living, breathing cause of a fight my family was always just on the verge of having. I'd never once thought about defending her, I guess, because I never imagined she needed protecting. I'd always seen her as tougher than I'd ever be. But in that moment, my first high buzzing through my body in a church parking lot, I saw her as just as vulnerable as I was. Instead of helping her, I'd used her as a uniting enemy with my parents to hide all the panic I felt over my impending coming out.

After the funeral, I didn't see my sister again for a few months. She stepped back into her routine, and I stepped back into mine. It didn't take long for me to completely throw the whole "oh, wow, she's always been my protector" aha moment out the window. I quickly returned to always siding with my parents in the ongoing feud between them.

Then one day, she returned.

I was home alone watching *The View* when my sister drove up. I was instantly annoyed because Bonnie Hunt was the guest, and I knew my sister would talk over her—well, my sister and every cohost on the show as well. Almost as important, though, I knew that the only reason my sister had shown up at our house again was because something was wrong.

"Hi," I said, flat and passive the way you sound when you're already pissed off at someone for talking over Bonnie Hunt. "What's going on?"

My sister looked flustered, rough, scared.

"Mom is on her way home. I called her and told her to get here because I need to talk to her."

I muted Bonnie. *Sorry, girl.*

"Why?" I asked, predicting the answer.

"I'm pregnant," she said, proving my instant prediction correct.

"Shit." I put aside my microwavable rice bowl, which was still frozen in the middle because I was and remain an impatient cook. "She's going to lose her mind—you realize that, right?"

My sister agreed as she paced the burgundy rug we'd spent our childhoods lying on watching *Drop Dead Fred*.

"We could soften the blow and also tell her I'm gay," I offered.

But my sister nixed this, saying with the type of precisely perfect timing you can only expect from impending doom (or Anjelica Huston in *The Addams Family*): "We'd kill her."

My mom's car came speeding up the driveway, and I turned off *The View* mid-episode. It was a day of firsts.

Basically, from that morning on, life at our house became the chaotic war zone it had been before my sister moved out. Everything my parents had been afraid of with my sister was coming true, and it only strengthened my role as the child they had nothing to worry about—a role there's no denying I relished. But the truth was, it could not have happened at a better time for me because I had just as secretly scandalous a life as my sister did, and when she moved back into the house, my own secret life became much easier to live behind everyone's distracted back.

This was the beginning of my tenure as an underage regular on hookup sites like Gay.com or Adam4Adam or XY. Seeing as I had convinced my parents to let me homeschool myself (more on this later), this was the bulk of my social life. And socialize I did, if you count sucking a stranger's dick in a McDonald's parking lot as "social"—which I do! Fast-food parking lots became my own version of Make-Out Point in a 1950s teen beach comedy *and* my own personal gay bathhouse sans the bath. No Bette Midler singing to a bunch of men in towels, but I could always count on having fries afterward. Plus one never ran the risk of running into Barry Manilow. I'd drive half an hour outside of town just to make out with a man I wasn't even attracted to in a Burger King parking lot, then do the same thing at a Wendy's the next morning, followed by a tryst at an Arby's that weekend. I wasn't eating the food, but I was certainly fast . . . and eating *something*. I had discovered the physical act of solidifying my gayness as opposed to harboring it as some vague concept, hidden on the bookshelf in my bedroom behind Ethan Mordden's Broadway history books. Taking the step of being gay in a literal and physical sense felt like finding the path leading to my true self. Also, it was really fun.

By the time I'd turned seventeen, I'd run out of guys within an hour's driving distance, and it was time to broaden my horizons. Luckily, my parents were so supportive of my dreams and so distracted with my sister's return that they let me start an internship in Atlanta at a regional theater.

At the time, my dad worked in the city half the week and rented a room in the apartment of an older woman who worked the night shift at the airport. When he wasn't there, I became this lady's roommate. She was a chain-smoking former hippie, with major Mama Cass vibes, whom I'd see smoking on her patio in the early morning light as I left for my internship and she got home from work. I'd ask her how her night had been, and she'd cough out, "Well, all the planes got off the ground, honey." This was the only moment we'd see each other all day in our odd little *Harold and Maude*–meets–*Friends* living arrangement.

The bulk of my theater internship was setting up cookies for purchase in the lobby, putting stamps on brochures, and scouring the internet for a guy to go on a real-life date with. Sure, I'd had my fair share of hookups in fast-food parking lots and even a few dorm rooms, but believe it or not, none of these experiences had ever been fulfilling. I was craving more. I wanted to go on a date. A real-life date.

Finally I found a twenty-year-old college sophomore who wasn't just cute but also six foot eight. You have never seen a seventeen-year-old boy take longer to pick out at an outfit from the Express for Men clearance rack, but finally—cargo pants and fitted tee found—I was going on a real-life date.

The guy, let's call him the Giant, picked the spot, which was an Indian restaurant in the ultra-groovy area of Little Five Points. As far as first dates between an insanely desperate seventeen-year-old who's lying about his age and pretending he's been on a date before but hasn't and a very hot, confident college sophomore go, it went pretty well. Besides being hot, he was also smart and studying art history, so I was mentally debating his ring size while he did most of the talking. The conversation was a stilted version of an improv game in which, instead of "Yes, and" I replied to everything with "Yes, you're right." He literally could've lit the building on fire, saying, "You are the one who lit this place on fire, Jeffery," and I would've agreed as I was escorted into a police car in handcuffs, shouting, "I love you," while they shut the door.

After dinner, he invited me back to his place, which filled me with the type of euphoric joy that turns some people into poets, some into mental patients, and some into both. I was leaving my body at the thought of him entering it, but I played it cool, pretending it was a slight inconvenience to my schedule before rabidly accepting. He told me to follow behind him, that it wasn't too far. I had, at this point, gotten to and around Atlanta without ever having driven onto a freeway in my life, because I was absolutely terrified and was by all accounts a terrible driver. Sure enough, though, it wasn't five minutes before I was following the Giant onto the bustling I-85, knuckles clinched onto the steering wheel in absolute terror. But there's a lesson there: if you're looking for a good way to get a seventeen-year-old gay boy to overcome his anxiety about driving, the sheer possibility of seeing what a six-foot-eight man's penis might look like is a good place to start.

By the time I'd arrived at his apartment, I was ready to rip my clothes off for the most romantic and adventurous sexual night of my life. Instead, I was greeted by the Giant, his slobbering dog, and eight of the Giant's friends from school who had come over to watch, discuss, and debate the extremely avant-garde French film *8 Women* by François Ozon in an orgy of stoned pretension. It was not the romantic and sexually adventurous evening with a six-foot-eight hottie I had imagined. Sure that movie is a musical, but it's in French, so I really don't think that counts. I kept trying to hold the guy's hand in the darkness before the TV because that's what people did on dates in movies. I was clumsy and clammy, and he couldn't have been less interested. All the while, however, I couldn't have been less interested in accepting that fact. I left fully in love and convinced he was as well, despite his showing zero sign of it. I lay awake that whole night imagining what it would have been like if he'd let me sleep over in his sheets, which I had creepily sniffed when going for a bathroom break somewhere in the midst of that tedious movie. When you can find romance in the stench of a college sophomore's unwashed sheets, you really know you're in trouble.

I returned to my family and the role of prodigal son the next day. Back home, the tension between my pregnant sister and my parents continued to escalate, while I stayed locked in my room obsessing over this stranger I had spent five hours with (mostly watching that stupid movie. Sorry to keep bringing it up, but if you make a *movie musical* called *8 Women*, it should be my absolute favorite thing that's ever existed. Hell, I'd even settle for seven women if the songs were better). I called, texted, and IM-ed the Giant nonstop the following week and got zero reply. Back home in my childhood bedroom and away from my pretend life in Atlanta, I was no longer playing it cool. The desperate seventeen-year-old homeschooler was out of hiding. Finally he replied to my hundreds of texts by telling me that he thought "we might want different things." Which is one of the nicest ways of saying, "Please leave me alone, you crazy bitch who sniffed my sheets while I wasn't looking."

A few more months of unfulfilling hookups passed as my sister got more and more pregnant and my family's shit show of conflict got shittier and shittier. All the while, the dynamic persisted: good son, bad daughter. And I more than contributed to keeping up this facade.

I got into a nightly chat routine with a cute musical theater major in Michigan that I met on Gay.com. We spent most of our time obsessing over the *Caroline, or Change* cast recording and trading blurry webcam dick pics. In other words, I was once again falling in love. I was desperate to meet this guy, go on a real-life date again, hook up, even sleep over, cuddle with someone for the first time, and yeah . . . sniff his sheets. Luckily my sister was extremely pregnant by now, and since everyone was focusing on that, no one batted an eye when I claimed I was driving a few hours to Tennessee to see a friend in a play but in actuality drove ten hours to Ann Arbor, Michigan, for sex with a stranger without telling a single soul where I was (besides the stranger I was going to see).

I drove it all in one shot, only pulling over to change the cast album CDs and piss. The dizzyingly free sensation of being entirely alone felt like living inside a Sufjan Stevens ballad, keeping me awake as I drove late into the night. Eventually I got to Michigan and finally did the type of thing I'd been dreaming of doing for so long: I went out to dinner with a cute guy, followed by sex, followed by cuddling in his bed watching the Carol Channing *Alice in Wonderland* TV movie as we drifted off to sleep. A much, much, much better choice than *8 Women*, thank you very much.

After roughly twenty-four hours, however, this veritable stranger and I had run out of things to talk about. You can only quote Tony Kushner lyrics about civil rights–era Louisiana at each other for so long. So we got stoned and went to see a double feature of *Howl's Moving Castle* and Nora Ephron's *Bewitched*, which is as sure a sign as any that you've hit a wall. With one full awkward day of small talk and sex left, the guy, let's call him Steve, suggested what any self-respecting twenty-year-old would have suggested to a seventeen-year-old he's stuck with because he just drove across the country to stay with him for the weekend: we decided to have a three-way with his best friend. Let's call him Rob.

I had never had a three-way before. Rob was hot, like next-level hot, and to make matters even more mind-boggling for my seventeen-year-old mind, he had been on Broadway as a child. I could barely look him in the eye when he passed me the bong, and when I dared do so, you could have opened an extremely niche and very sticky water park in my underwear.

The beginning of that afternoon's three-way remains a blur. Multiple bong rips and one's first experience of making out with a hot guy in Calvin Klein briefs for the first time will do that. But what the beginning lacks in clarity, the middle and conclusion more than make up for in horror. Things had just gotten very hot and heavy when I felt rumblings in my stomach, that familiar overture announcing the beginning of a golden-age musical comedy called *GI Distress*. I broke into an awful sweat. My tongue halfway down Steve's throat, I tried to push the unavoidable out of my reality, begging my body to calm down and wait, to give me ten minutes. *You monster of a digestive tract, don't you see I'm just beginning my very first three-way?! Have you no shame?!*

But we all know how these things go, and there was absolutely no waiting. The bathroom was aggressively close to the bed, the door practically serving as a footboard. There was no way I'd be able to get what I needed to get done without anyone noticing, which, albeit new to three-way sex, I suspected might put a slight if not literal damper on the overall mood.

I excused myself as casually as possible, locking the door behind me, and immediately went into a full-blown panic. I paced the two or three feet between the toilet and the shower, my mind racing, Steve and Rob continuing to hook up outside, my stomach growling like a trapped opossum under your porch, my dick still somehow hard like I was on a fistful of Viagra.

All the while, I kept thinking, *I drove to Michigan for THIS?!*

Then I thought of the old "turn on the shower to drown out the noise" trick. I flipped on the faucet, which is the most obvious way to let anyone know you're shitting next to announcing, "I'm going to go take a big ole dump now. See ya soon! It's gonna stink!" In an attempt to pass it off, I called out to the guys "I'm just going to rinse off real quick!"

I collapsed onto the toilet and did my business, the prior overture of stomach rumbling now launching into a full-on four-act opera of epic and tragic proportions. Tosca was leaping from her balcony and directly into the toilet bowl, over and over and over. My face pulsed a shameful heat that I could feel not just on my cheeks but inside them. And not just the ones on my face. Drumroll, bong rip, cymbal clash. I'd also absent-mindedly turned the shower on to hot, and if there had been any question of this apartment's hot water pressure, it was immediately answered by the clouds of steam that filled the room and began to blind me. I couldn't even see my hand reaching for wad after wad of toilet paper. It was like a community theater production of *Fiddler on the Roof* with the fog machine on full blast for Fruma Sarah's entrance.

That was when I tried to flush and realized the toilet was clogged. Very, very clogged. Unable to see what I was doing, I had stuffed the toilet full of toilet paper and, well, the other stuff too. In a frenzy, I grabbed a plunger and plunged with all my might, but all that achieved was getting water and grotesque balls of soiled toilet paper onto the linoleum.

I lifted the lid on the back of the toilet and fucked around with the weird ball on a stick lever and chain thing that absolutely no one who's not a plumber has ever understood. But it wasn't working. Nothing was working. Which was when my eyes fell upon the window above the toilet. Light bulb. My eyes went back to the toilet, then back to the window, then back to the toilet.

There are moments in life where you are faced with a decision: You can either turn off the scalding and steaming shower, gather yourself together, open the door to your very first three-way with two hot guys you barely know, and announce you've blocked the toilet with your own poo-poo. Or you can open the window and throw fistfuls of your own feces and toilet paper onto the lawn below. It took me roughly two seconds to make my choice.

The window was only slightly difficult to pry open, and when I did so, the steam rushed out as if the steam itself couldn't handle the smell of my shit. The fresh air brushed against my sweaty face as I took a deep, uncontaminated breath, shoved my hand into the toilet, grabbed a horrific wad, and began to throw. I tried not to look at what I was touching but instead entered into a trancelike state of grabbing, throwing, grabbing, throwing. Finally the toilet flushed, and the clearest, most beautiful water filled the basin. You could've drunk the stuff! I didn't but hypothetically one could have if one were super thirsty or kinky. I jumped into the shower for obvious reasons, specifically to scrub my hands until they were practically raw, before returning to the three-way as if nothing had happened.

Rob and Steve and I got back to business as the sun set on a beautiful Midwestern summer day. I'd gotten away with my ruse, and as my first three-way came to its momentous conclusion, I thought to myself, *I drove to Michigan for THIS*.

Perhaps it was some sort of karmic retribution, because as I was throwing my own shit out the window, my sister (whose bike I had covered in dog shit all those years before) went into labor. When my mom called to tell me, I panicked, seeing as I was allegedly just a hop and a skip over in Tennessee and not ten hours away in Michigan. I had to make up an excuse about not being able to get there until the morning, blaming the fact that I didn't want to drive at night. Then I bid the two hot guys goodbye, got into my car, and drove all night long until I arrived at the hospital the next morning.

As I sat in the waiting room, attempting to hide a hickey on my neck that had come from either Steve or Rob, the role of "golden child" felt as false as it ever had. I could've come clean to my parents, admitted that my constant performance as a trustworthy kid was false, that I was just as fucked-up as my sister, and that I was just better at getting away with it. I could have accepted accountability for all the times I'd used her as a punch line just to make myself look better. I could have stood up for my brave and courageous sister, pointed out how incredibly she had turned her life around the second she discovered her pregnancy, how tough and tenacious she was and had always been, how this baby was bringing us all together again in ways none of us could ever have predicted, that we should set aside the roles we'd given ourselves and step into a future of truthful imperfection, how this was the day our collective healing as a family could finally begin.

But I was too distracted to do any of that. My mind kept roaming back to Steve in Michigan and the letter that would have likely appeared on his door sometime that day: a letter complaining about the piles of shit and toilet paper that had rained down from his bathroom around three the previous afternoon, creating a grotesque and tragic little snowman beneath his window.

But to all of them—my sister, my parents, Rob, Steve, Steve's landlord, the Giant, and every other mess I'd made—I said nothing. Instead I sat back, savoring my place as the good son. The golden child. The one who always did things right.

All the while thinking, *I'm sorry. I'm sorry for all my shit.*

# No Names, No Names

I once stole a VHS copy of the Harvey Fierstein movie *Torch Song Trilogy*—unfortunately not in some sort of intricate heist situation involving *Mission: Impossible*–style pullies and a ticking bomb inside a nearby VHS of Paul Rudnick's *In and Out* from an uber-gay Blockbuster but instead from a kind college theater professor who my family met at church one Sunday. I can't recall why we were at church because it wasn't something we did that often by the time I was in high school, but there we were at our local Episcopalian chapel when a tall man in trendy glasses and a cute outfit walked over to our breakfast table.

"I hear I need to meet the Selfs," this dapper man said, extending his manicured hand to my already dazzled mom as he introduced himself.

I was immediately invigorated, embarrassed, nervous, and enthralled by this man's mere presence. I was fifteen and still closeted to just about everyone I knew, aside from a few friends, and I was always on a combination of code red alert and pure euphoria when around an obviously gay person. My inner thoughts usually went something like this: *Can he smell it on me? I hope he can't smell it on me. Actually no, I do hope he can smell it on me. Please, sir, I beg of you—smell me!*

I had always known I was gay. There was never a moment of self-awakening or a big aha to my true identity. I came out of my mother's womb with a deep and preternatural understanding that I was attracted to boys and musical comedies with strong female leads.

One of my earliest memories is of watching soap operas while eating chopped-up hot dogs (irony) as early as four and getting baby boners from the bare-chested heartthrobs on the screen. This was the late eighties and early nineties, so it wasn't exactly something I was broadcasting to my family. But then again, nobody was batting an eye at my nightly performances as Miss Hannigan from *Annie*, clutching an empty bottle of Southern Comfort I'd pulled out of the garbage, still haunted by the aromatic apparitions of cheap whiskey, and wearing one of the wigs from a tattered cardboard box full of fake hair I'd made my mom buy me at a yard sale.

The majority of gay role models in my town were pretty bleak. One man was named Sidney Guy Johnson, the type of name you should've found in the credits of a William Wyler movie and not belonging to a lonely man in a small southern town that didn't fully appreciate him. He was the typical pathologically lying alcoholic with long-ago dreams dropped into the wastebasket of reality that you often find acting or directing at your local community theater. My mom and I were obsessed with him.

Multiple nights a week, the phone would ring just as we were sitting down to dinner.

"Jeeeeeeeeffffffferrrrrryyyyy," he'd drawl and slur at once. "Is NANcyyyyyy there?" He couldn't have been more southern, gay, and drunk if he'd been hooked up to an IV of mint juleps while brushing the hair of a Madame Alexander Scarlett O'Hara doll. Which he very well might have been.

My mom would stay on the phone with him well into the night, listening to his drunken rambling. When my dad would complain about these hijacked evenings, she would express her loving compassion for poor old Sidney.

"He's so alone, Scott. I'm probably one of the only people he has to talk to," she'd explain, and she was probably right. Sidney had no loved ones checking in on him, but he often claimed he had once had a family of his own until his wife and daughter were killed in a tragic car accident. Few ever believed him, but no one ever called him out on it either, because people pitied gin-soaked Sidney, who looked close to eighty years old even though he was barely fifty-five. And who could be surprised? That was simply what you expected to happen to "men like that."

The tall professor in trendy glasses from church was different. He was openly gay, handsome, in his midthirties, and had a good job, nice clothes, and a fancy car. He quickly took me under his wing, let me sit in on his college theater classes, and would hire me to feed his cats when he went out of town on one of the envious vacations he was always taking with his worldly gay friends.

On one of those occasions I snooped around in his bedroom, finding a cabinet of BelAmi gay porn tapes and the aforementioned VHS copy of *Torch Song Trilogy*. I may have paused to briefly enjoy the fruits of the former find, but it was the latter that I pocketed. I may have been a hormonal teenager, but I understood my cultural priorities. And as I watched that movie over and over—eventually expanding to others like *To Wong Foo*, *Jeffrey*, and *Longtime Companion*—I began to understand my deep-seated need to connect to and join the tribe of gay men who went before me. I would stay up, night after night when the coast was clear, watching these movies over and over, dreaming of being an out gay man in New York City with a community to fit into.

Finding that tribe would be my number one goal for the next few years.

When I was in high school, my parents would let me go to New York all by myself and stay with one of the people we'd gotten to know from a summer stock theater company that had come to our town a few years prior. Her name was Corinne, and she was the type of responsible and lovely person my parents could trust to not let me go too wild in the Big Apple. I'd save up my money from working at the Barnes & Noble Cafe and babysitting, then take the sixteen-hour Amtrak ride from Atlanta to New York's Penn Station because I was afraid of flying.

I would spend all my money on student rush tickets to shows, cramming eight or sometimes more performances into my short trip. Though *Torch Song Trilogy* had closed before I was born, the shows I was most drawn to were either gay-related or gay-created. These trips to the city were some of the greatest experiences of my life, and every time I boarded the train to go home, I was distraught with the feeling of this whole world slipping away before I could barely even touch its grimily glamorous surface. I needed a connection to that world more than absolutely anything else. So I did what all teenage boys do when they reach a certain age: I started writing fan letters to successful gay guys working on Broadway.

One such letter was to the late actor Gary Beach. I had just seen his Tony Award–winning performance in *The Producers* and was completely mesmerized by him. He had the type of star power that felt like it was from another generation, oozing funny, showbiz, and (most important to me) gay. On the train back to Georgia, I read all my Playbills cover to cover and discovered that he'd starred as Lumière in the original production of *Beauty and the Beast*, which my family had seen on my first-ever trip to New York very early in the show's run. When I got home and found his name in my old *Beauty and the Beast* Playbill, I decided it was some sort of universal sign that he should be my friend. So I wrote him a letter.

A few weeks passed before a very elegant envelope arrived with the return address of Broadway's St. James Theatre, and I knew exactly who it was from. I opened the letter carefully so as to not rip the ornate stationery, which had the name of its sender embossed across the top, and read a short but very kind response thanking me for my note and wishing me luck on my theatrical pursuits. It wasn't some monumental exchange between the two of us in which he imparted wisdom that would change the trajectory of my life, but the sheer fact that this out gay man living in the city I longed to be a part of had sent me a letter direct from the dressing room at the St. James Theatre was more than enough to shift something inside me. Just touching the expensive-looking paper made me feel that much closer to my tribe.

Cut to four years later. I had just dropped out of (coincidentally) Gary Beach's alma mater, the University of North Carolina School of the Arts (a saga we'll get to later) and had moved to New York. I was nineteen and had finally done it: I was really and truly a gay guy living in New York City. I had gotten a job handing out flyers advertising the musical *The Drowsy Chaperone*, which was apparently desperate enough to sell tickets that they had a crew of aimless youth like myself standing in Times Square throughout a brutal heat wave stopping people to confusingly announce, "It may be hot out here but it's freezing inside at *The Drowsy Chaperone*."

It was very quickly clear that I was not cut out for handing out flyers on the street. Being outside wasn't necessarily "my thing," and I hated (and still hate) speaking to strangers—or most people, for that matter. So after only a few days I developed the routine of picking up the flyers, going to get a sandwich at Subway, and finding a shady spot to sit and read near enough to my post that I could get there if anyone started looking for me.

One day I was sitting on the ground in Shubert Alley, the mythic Broadway alleyway between Forty-Fourth and Forty-Fifth Streets, connecting two of the busiest streets of jewel box theaters. I'd just finished my sandwich when I looked up and . . . oh my God . . . saw none other than Gary Beach! My first New York celebrity sighting, and he was someone I had exchanged letters with! Now, here he was walking south to work for his

Wednesday matinee. In a demonstration of the type of gusto that makes nineteen-year-olds both admirable and unbearable all at once, I ran over to him.

"I'm so sorry to bother you, but I'm a huge fan. My name is Jeffery, and I wrote you a letter a few years ago and . . ."

Before I could finish, he flashed his big, magically theatrical, star-powered smile and cut me off.

"From Rome, Georgia?" He let out a baritone chuckle. "What the heck are you doing in New York?"

I explained that I'd just dropped out of school and moved to the city and was figuring out what I was going to do next. I casually explained how I was trying to get into stand-up comedy, writing musicals, filmmaking, acting, sketch comedy, directing theater, producing performance art, and writing a novel.

"Well, it sounds like you're pretty busy," he said after my monologue of precociousness. "But if you ever have time, drop off your info at the stage door, and we can grab a meal between shows one of these afternoons. Have you ever been to Joe Allen's?"

I had not, but I'd read enough gossipy Broadway history books to know that Joe Allen's was a restaurant on Forty-Sixth Street that was the unofficial city hall of the Broadway community. Its walls were lined with the posters of infamous Broadway flops, and it served the best meat loaf in New York. When I revealed just how theatrically informed I was, he lit up like the marquees that surrounded us.

"Drop off your information, and we'll do it!"

With that he continued bouncing along to his theater, where he'd go through the unassuming stage door, put on his costume, and star on fucking Broadway in a role he'd won a Tony for a couple of years prior. My head was reeling as I tossed my stack of *Drowsy Chaperone* flyers into the trash and headed home to savor what had just occurred.

After recounting this whole experience to a friend that night, I decided not to drop my information off at the stage door. My friend had a good point: older gay Broadway star runs into nineteen-year-old fan in a literal alley and invites him to dinner after a five-minute conversation. We all know where that gay personal essay ends up. So I jotted the whole magical encounter down in my journal and continued to hone my impressive skills of procrastination.

Over the following weeks, I continued my job of "handing out" flyers and proselytizing about the cold air inside the walls of *The Drowsy Chaperone*'s Marquis Theatre, but I was still approaching it with whatever is tremendously less than half-assed attention. I'd started bringing a notebook and was killing time by writing a solo show while I sat on the toilet in the bathrooms that used to be open to the public at the Marriot Marquis lobby but have since been made just for guests. Perhaps because random nineteen-year-olds used to spend all day in their stalls writing solo shows instead of getting butts in seats of the actual Broadway show they were being paid to help advertise.

After a couple of weeks, the "chaperone" of *The Drowsy Chaperone*'s marketing team caught on to my bullshit. I was sitting at my desk—aka atop the lobby toilet as I'd done for days at this point—when my flip phone rang.

"Jeffery?" the marketing lady who had hired me hissed.

"Uh-huh."

"Where are you?" she asked, her voice giving way to the fact she was clearly already aware that the answer was most certainly *not* outside at my post in Times Square handing out flyers to people who never once had had an interest in flyers.

"Using the bathroom real quick," I said with the ease of someone who'd just taken a long, refreshing piss. Which I had. "I'll be right back out in a minute."

She cleared her throat, and my heart began to pound. I hated confrontation almost as much as I hated handing flyers to strangers or being outside.

"One of the show's producers has walked by the theater five times today, and they have yet to see you once."

To which I had the audacity to say, "Really?! Well, that's very odd."

"He says he didn't see you yesterday, either."

I felt my face burning as I nervously fidgeted, pulling sheet after sheet of toilet paper off the roll. Between the discarded flyers and now the toilet paper, it would be safe to wonder why the hell I was so determined to waste the Marriot Marquis's paper-based resources.

"Jeffery, do you really think you're the first person to try and screw us over at this job? When you came in for your interview, you seemed like a really nice kid and I was excited to help you out, but this is very, very disappointing."

I wanted to crawl directly into the toilet and disappear, but besides that being a disgusting idea, the toilet was now completely full of the unsoiled toilet paper I'd been yanking off its roll.

"Well, I've been a little sick and . . ."

"You're fired." *Click*.

I hurried out of the theater lobby in such shame. I had worn my required *Drowsy Chaperone* T-shirt to work that day and kept looking over my shoulder manically as I descended the escalator back to the street. I was petrified that I'd be spotted by the producer who had turned me in for being a total deadbeat at my first job in the city and who was sure to blacklist me from show business for the rest of time. Luckily, I made it the few blocks west to a friend's apartment, where I changed shirts, got stoned, and tried to forget all about what a jerk I'd been to do that with my job.

I walked back to the subway to head back to where I was staying in Washington Heights. Inside the train, I was crammed in a corner as the A Express pulled out of the station. Attempting to adjust the strap of my bag, I accidentally elbowed someone standing behind me.

"Sorry!" I said as the person turned around, revealing it was none other than . . . I gasped: "Gary Beach?!"

"All right, cut the shit. Are you stalking me?" He said it in a way that might or might not have been a joke, and then he smiled. "You never dropped your information off at the stage door."

This was, I would soon learn, very Gary Beach. He was from another era, the type of person who still had a landline, who still used a phone book, and who still said things like "drop your information off at the stage door." I explained that I thought his offering to have dinner sometime was just his being nice, to which he abruptly cut me off with a laugh. "Oh, Jeffery, I am not nice."

We were nearing his subway stop when he pulled out a business card (like I said, another era) and told me his partner had just had them made. The card simply stated his name and home phone number.

"Call me!" he sang as the doors opened and he stepped out onto the Columbus Circle platform.

Was my friend right? Was Gary Beach just going to be some handsy older man with a thing for naive nineteen-year-olds who spend a great deal of time in public restrooms? But upon considering all of that, I still really wanted to go to Joe Allen's for the first time, so I figured that there was only one way to find out. I called and we made plans to meet at his theater between shows the following Wednesday, where he'd show me around backstage before walking over to the restaurant for an early dinner.

I arrived in the theater district that Wednesday afternoon a full two hours early for fear of being late. I wandered the west Forties past all the theaters where I could hear the orchestras and bits of shows seeping through the closed doors. I'd been inside Broadway theaters but certainly never backstage, and everything about that particular afternoon was feeling borderline religious. Finally it was time for *The Producers* matinee to end, and I hovered across the street like a creep at a playground as the audience poured out. People formed a crowd around the stage door to await exiting cast members for photos and autographs, and I felt like the hottest of shit when I sauntered up, telling the guard my name and that I was there to see Gary Beach. I was told to wait as various sweaty cast members made their way past me onto the sidewalk to greet cheering fans. I stood a few feet from the wings of the St. James Theatre, with the *Producers* set pieces stored in every available corner, the giant office scenery dangling in the air, the empty stage itself peeking out through a part in the curtains. This was the same St. James Theatre where the original *Oklahoma!* premiered, where Carol Channing starred in the original run of *Hello, Dolly!*, and where I would soon learn Gary made his own Broadway debut replacing Clifford David in the original production of *1776*.

Finally I was called up to Gary's dressing room.

"Welcome to Broadway!" he declared, drying his wet hair. The dressing room was small and cramped, with its ancient muck impossible to hide despite the expensive lamps, rugs, and curtains that had been installed for its star. It was the most glamorous place I'd ever seen. Gary introduced me to his dresser, who was getting things ready for the second show of the day, arranging a rack of Gary's costumes. I fell into a trance as my eyes scanned the Chrysler Building–inspired evening gown he wore for his first entrance along with the full-on Hitler uniform for act 2.

"Hungry?" Gary asked.

On our way out, Gary led me onto the empty stage, which was lit by the single-bulb ghost light that's placed in the corner of all Broadway theaters when a show isn't happening. We stopped dead center and looked out at the sea of empty seats. I thought about all the history that had happened on the very spot I was standing, and I wanted Gary to take my picture really badly, but I only had my flip phone and I was too embarrassed to ask. In a blur, we left through the stage door where a handful of excited fans greeted Gary with their Playbills and Sharpies before we continued on our way back through Shubert Alley down to Joe Allen's.

Joe Allen's is on the basement level of an old brownstone on Restaurant Row. It's got that rarefied aesthetic that can only be described as "Old New York": a low-ceilinged storm cellar of Gatsbyesque charm. The waiter dropped off the menus as Gary promptly ordered a martini.

"After this long a run, I could do the show under anesthesia, and frankly, if it runs any longer, I might have to," he said with a grin.

I wanted to order a drink as well, hoping the waiter would not ask me for an ID. People rarely did in New York during this time. If I ordered the drink, I would have to lie and claim to be twenty-one . . . *but how many more times was I going to see this guy anyway?* I thought. I confidently lied about my age and ordered a pinot noir.

Gary pointed out various show posters on the wall, explaining that every poster decorating Joe Allen's was from an infamously terrible Broadway flop.

"And I've been in three of them!" he said, beaming with pride.

All I had to do was ask "Which ones?" and we were off to the races. And by races I mean a tap dancing marathon of Gary's showbiz musings and gossip from his forty-plus-year career. As I would quickly learn, Gary loved nothing more than regaling an interested listener with his perfectly timed tales of Broadway past. And in me, he had found the most captive and eager audience of a lifetime.

He told me about his many years of playing Rooster in the original run of *Annie*, in which he acted opposite a slew of names that would make any show queen quiver: Dorothy Loudon, Alice Ghostley, Jane Connell—names that likely register nothing for many people but for folks like me are essentially saints. He told me about how, when he heard through the backstage grapevine that former movie star Betty Hutton was coming out of retirement to audition for the show one afternoon while the theater was empty, he hid in the balcony to watch as this former Paramount Pictures contract player read the audition scene with a stage manager and sang "Little Girls" with the pianist through her nervous tears. He told me about a secret door in the back of the Palace Theatre, which had been installed for Judy Garland to make her entrance during her concerts there, where he would stand and smoke cigarettes while dressed as a literal candlestick between scenes of *Beauty and the Beast*. He told me about his year touring with Carol Channing and Mary Martin in James Kirkwood's doomed play *Legends!* and how on a weekend off, he went to Palm Springs with a list of "must dos" given to him by Mary Martin. She told him all about "the best restaurant in the world," and when he arrived, excited to give it a try, he discovered it was a Chinese restaurant in a strip mall with bottles of ketchup on the folding tables. Gary said he looked around and thought, "Well, this says more about Mary Martin than I care to know."

His showbiz stories went back long before his own career started. He told me about when, as a teenager, he went to see Carol Channing in her return to the original run of *Hello, Dolly!* The audience was eagerly awaiting showtime when an announcement interrupted everyone's buzz to say, "This evening the role of Dolly Levi will not be played by Carol Channing." Everyone in the place groaned, seats squeaking as people got up to make their way to the box office for refunds . . . before the announcement continued, "At this performance the role will be played by . . . Ethel Merman."

Miss Merman was set to start the following week to close the show's run and was making a surprise performance a few days early. The audience went nuts, obviously.

The mention of Ethel Merman led to Gary telling the story of sitting in the balcony when he was around my age, just as fresh and hopeful as I was at that very moment, watching Merman and Mary Martin perform their history-making two-person concert. As he described them dressed in their Dolly Levi gowns, coming down side-by-side staircases to that famous score, he got this look that I would eventually learn was Gary at his most emotionally clicked in, his rawest honesty. His eyes turned glassy, his gaze became lightning focused, and overcome, he would inevitably start to cry. Over the coming years, I would hear this story an endless number of times . . . and it never ceased to move either one of us.

By the end of that meal, I felt like I'd known Gary my whole life, likely because I'd been waiting my whole life to meet someone like him. A few weeks later, he invited me to dinner between shows again, this time bringing along his very lovely husband, Jeff. I would imagine Jeff wanted to sniff out the twink his husband was buying meat loaf for (not a euphemism), but there was no way to tell because he was so endlessly kind and welcoming. Gary and Jeff had been together since 1987, when they met doing a San Francisco run of *Les Misérables*. That was also the year of my birth, but I bit my tongue before adding this detail because I was now in a star-crossed romance with Joe Allen's house pinot noir that I didn't want my underaged status to come between. Gary and Jeff were beautiful together, so at ease, so amused by one another, and profoundly in love. They were the first gay couple I'd ever met who made me think, *Oh, it can be like that.*

By the end of the summer, they were having me over for home-cooked meals, and eventually they even invited me to their house in the Pines on Fire Island. I had never been to that gay beach oasis before, but being a gay kid obsessed with being a gay man when I grew up, I knew what the Pines was like, and it more than lived up to my expectations. It was offseason when I went for the first time in early October, and the trains and ferry required to get out there ran on a very limited schedule. Gary had given me detailed instructions about which train to get from Penn Station, when to transfer, where to get off, and where to get the shuttle to the boat. I diligently wrote it all down and proceeded to get completely lost somewhere in the dregs of Long Island. I'd brought along a friend, a guy I had a crush on and was hoping to impress, but he was new to the city too and was no help with figuring out the logistics of the journey. Dead set on not turning back and giving up, I caved, called a taxi at whatever train station I'd ended up at, and forked out two hundred bucks to get to the dock. I was going to Gary Beach's house on Fire fucking Island if it was the last thing I did. It was also my last two hundred dollars, but I'd recently opened a slew of credit cards that I was maxing out like it was my job, which I suppose it sort of was. I vowed I'd figure the money thing out later . . . and I'm still figuring it out to this day, by the way, in case you have any suggestions.

Gary and Jeff greeted us at the ferry and welcomed the guy I'd brought along as lovingly as if he weren't a total stranger tagging along with some kid they'd only known for four months. We headed down the creaky wooden boardwalks into the dense forest dotted with houses. The island was completely silent, just the crisp fall air that mixed with the sea breeze, and deer and squirrels rustling behind the trees. There are no cars in the Pines on Fire Island; the wooden sidewalks are built roughly five feet off the ground and snake through the tiny community. As we walked, Gary directed our attention to the houses with the type of historical backgrounds he knew I'd get a kick out of.

"That one is Jerry Herman's place. That's what writing *Hello, Dolly!*, *Mame*, and *La Cage* can buy you," Gary lectured as he pointed out a very large, opulent mansion. Then he turned to a more modest cabin and added, "And that one belongs to the guy who wrote *Nunsense*."

Later, when we made our way through the sandy woods to the equally gay community next door called Cherry Grove, he explained that the forest between the two is called the Meat Rack; it's where guys have always gone to cruise and hook up. Back in the day, he expounded, the Sayville Police Department would come across the bay to the Pines and hide out in the Meat Rack to bust gay guys having public sex.

"These cops would hide out in the bushes, waiting until it was crowded. Then, just as everything was getting hot and heavy, all at once the cops would flip on their flashlights, sending all the half-naked gay guys running in all directions away from the bust." His voice became more and more serious as he went on: "Story goes that one gay guy pushed another gay guy and shouted, 'Out of my way, Mary,' to which the other guy cried, 'No names! No names!'"

This is what life with Gary Beach would always be like. Wonderful stories told wonderfully by a truly wonderful man. As the months went by, I spent more and more time with Gary and Jeff. Besides their house on Fire Island, they had a beautiful old house in Milford, Pennsylvania, where they brought me up to stay for Thanksgiving and New Year's.

Usually I brought along whomever I was sleeping with or trying to sleep with at that particular time, even when Gary and Jeff had never met the person. One such guy, named Pete, was matinee idol handsome and kind, if slightly performative. On our first cozy night in Milford, Pete made a big deal about going on a jog the next morning despite the fact that we'd all stayed up well past midnight guzzling vodka tonics and watching clips of 1970s Mitzi Gaynor specials. Both of those things can really take it out of a person, and I would have sawed off my own feet with a butter knife before going on a jog that next morning. But sticking to his slightly performative word, a queasy-looking Pete took off on an early morning run, assuring all of us that he'd be back in an hour to shower before the lunch reservations our hosts had made. Gary warned Pete that it was very easy to get lost in the area.

"Write the address down," Gary instructed, but cool, calm, assured Pete insisted he'd remember.

"Trust me. I have great navigation," he promised as Gary glared at me from across our bowls of cereal with a look that suggested he didn't believe it.

An hour passed as Gary, Jeff, and I slowly filled our bodies with enough coffee to get moving. Then another hour as we all got showered and ready for lunch. Still no Pete. After three hours, everyone was hungry, annoyed, and worried. This was a very rustic area with many forests in which to get lost or devoured by a bear, so we decided it was probably time to drive around and look for him or whatever was left of his half-eaten corpse. Gary and Jeff wondered aloud about the process of reporting a missing person while I seethed to myself for inviting Pete in the first place. *He's not even that hot*, I fumed to myself . . . even though, let's be real, he was.

Finally, we rounded a corner in the middle of truly nowhere and discovered a terrified-looking Pete at the end of the road. His sweaty, fearful face melted into utter relief the moment he saw us, then he slowly walked toward the car.

"Oh, so now he *doesn't* need to run?" Gary deadpanned.

We all managed to get over the annoyance enough to have a nice lunch, but I noticed Gary glare at Pete in a way I'd never seen him glare at anyone. He would look slyly over at me and sigh when Pete said something particularly annoying.

After lunch, we walked into an antique store on the adorable high street, where Pete promptly knocked over an entire shelf of mugs, all of them shattering at his feet. Gary turned on his heels and bolted out of the store saying, under his breath, "Did I just hear the stage manager call places?"

Needless to say, I didn't continue seeing Pete when we returned to the city. A month later, however, he sent Gary and Jeff a very kind note thanking them for having us out to the house . . . and sent it to the wrong address.

My relationship with Gary and Jeff continued over my first few years living in New York City, which also turned out to be Gary and Jeff's final few years living in New York City. Our friendship wasn't even thwarted when the thing I had dreaded for years finally happened and Gary realized I had lied to him about my age when we first met. Or rather merely avoided it ever coming up to begin with. He was playing Thénardier in a revival of *Les Misérables* and a fuck buddy of mine who was understudying Marius blew my cover by mentioning that he had just attended my twenty-first birthday party. When the Understudy Marius told me what happened, I dreaded seeing Gary again. However, the next time we had dinner, he simply placed his hand on mine and said, "I know you lied to me, and I get why you lied to me. But just don't do it again." Then we clinked our (now totally legal for me) martinis together.

After a hip replacement and a lifetime on Broadway, Gary was ready to retire and do absolutely nothing. He and Jeff moved to West Palm Beach, and I didn't see them for a couple of years. I moved to LA and had started dating a guy named Patrick, who would become my boyfriend for two years. At this particular point, the relationship had begun speeding down a hill, a hill whose blades of toxic grass we were still clinging to in the final bitter weeks when Gary and Jeff happened to be in LA visiting.

We'd made plans to have dinner with them, but the car Patrick and I shared overheated on our way. We screamed at each other for roughly an hour before finally getting a cab that we couldn't afford across town to the dinner with Gary and Jeff (and, oddly enough, the Understudy Marius who'd previously revealed my real age and who had remained a friend). Up until that night, I really and truly believed I would somehow make our rapidly disintegrating relationship work: I would be one half of an unhappy couple with a super hot guy who could sometimes make me smile and the rest of the time had really, really nice biceps. We slapped on our closest approximations of happy faces for the dinner, but sitting across from Gary, I noticed him give my boyfriend that same glare he'd given Pete after he got lost on his jog. And something clicked. Whatever toxic thing this relationship had become was nothing like the in-sync joy I'd first noticed between Gary and Jeff all those years ago. Of course, by the time we'd made it home, I had buried any such realization as far down into my subconscious as it could go . . . which is impressively far, by the way. But eventually, a week later, the relationship finally blew up for good, and I absolutely lost my mind and documented my every self-sabotaging step on social media—an epic saga of mental illness that we will get into later.

In the midst of this madcap showcase of my instability, Gary reached out to say he wanted me to hop on a plane and come spend a week with him and Jeff in Florida—their treat. He didn't ask questions or elaborate on his obvious concerns; he just offered a solution for helping me feel better. I got on a plane a few days later and spent seven magnificent days in their care. They nursed me back to some form of health with home-cooked meals, vodka, swimming, golf cart rides, and even a Zumba class, which I took with Jeff and the over-sixty-year-old women who lived in their gated community. By the time I returned to LA, I might not have been fixed, but what had been an inner symphony of debilitating despair had become a cozier four-piece jazz combo of manageable moodiness.

Years passed, and I moved on to other relationships, finally ending up with my husband, Augie. Gary and Jeff relocated to Palm Springs, where they always had belonged in the first place, which gave them a chance to get to know Augie over the years before we eventually got married. The second-to-last time I saw Gary was at our wedding. It was a packed crowd with people standing in any available corner they could find because we are both codependent people pleasers who over-invited and because we forgot to make a list of RSVPs. I was oddly nervous for someone who loves attention, but other than the spectacle of the wedding itself, I couldn't help but grapple with the intense feeling that I was getting legit motherfucking married. Gary and Jeff were seated close to the front of the room, and as I tearfully made my way through my speech, I looked out into the crowd and locked eyes with Gary. I couldn't help but think about the time he first introduced me to Jeff and how it was the first moment I ever saw what a truly committed, long-term gay relationship looked like. His eyes stared at me, emotional and lightning focused, red as Dolly Levi's gown, and shedding the type of glassy tears I'd seen so many times before. It was the way his face would transform when telling a story that meant the world to him. A Mary-Martin-and-Ethel-Merman-descending-rival-staircases-for-one-night-only-on-Broadway type of expression. And from his proud and encouraging and emotional presence, my gut and heart told me that I was making the right decision.

Gary died a few months later, and it will never not matter to me that he was there the day Augie and I tied the knot. That he met my parents, my friends, my in-laws, my world. I sometimes wonder what would have become of me if I'd bailed on that dinner with Gary. If I'd gone through those early New York years without someone like Gary rooting me on. When I think about this, I inevitably get furious because there was a whole generation, a whole tribe of men like Gary, a tribe that never got the chance to be the type of friend that Gary was to my young self. We all deserve that type of mentor: men from that same gay New York City tribe I spent my childhood dreaming of joining, the type of men I watched over and over in my stolen VHS of *Torch Song Trilogy*. Men who loved to tell the types of stories that people like me yearn to hear all these years later. Men who had been there, on the ground, before being gay was what it is today. Somehow Gary survived his generation's plague; his draft number never getting picked to call him to the battlegrounds of that terrible time. But so many of his friends did not, and the void they left remains glaringly vacant.

One time I asked Gary about what it was like during those early days of the AIDS crisis, and he told me to imagine ten friends and then said eight of them would be dead by the end of the month. He would reminisce about weekly funerals and memorials, about running into countless handsome men who had aged fifty years in a week's time, about his brilliant colleagues who were excelling in their field or just on the cusp of getting to try . . . all there one day and gone the next. He carried them with him and never once took for granted his lucky privilege of somehow weathering that horrible storm of an era. He embodied a lost generation that changed the world but had endlessly more magic to make.

I was so lucky to have had a Gary in my life; his friendship influenced just about everything about me. I continue to wonder just how different a world this would be if more Garys had survived. If guys of that generation had gotten to stick around and the tribe was still full, I suspect things would be a lot more joyful, colorful, loving, and creative. Perhaps every young scared-out-of-his-depth gay boy new to the city would find a loving support system like the one I had, and maybe, just maybe, the big gay world would be a better place. Or at the very least, a place with better modern musical comedies.

Through meeting Gary, I discovered the power of having a tribe. Sure it was missing a lot of its tribesmen, but I found a part of what was left in Gary after so many stories were washed away like the dunes of Fire Island itself. So I cling to the tales that remain. Like Gary's old Fire Island "Out of my way, Mary" anecdote because they're the things that can still connect the then to the now.

"Out of my way, Mary!" some gay boy fresh off the Amtrak shouts as he charges ahead to the future that awaits him, with the ghosts of all the tribesmen who came and went before rooting him forward, shouting back in unison, "No names! No names!"

# Ten Further Reasons Not to Sabotage Your Life

1. The smell of my dog's paws.
2. The audacity of Barbra Streisand's 1994 Anaheim concert.
3. Listening to Elizabeth Ashley's recording of the Tennessee Williams biography by John Lahr as you walk down any beach whatsoever but especially Provincetown.
4. Calvin Klein underwear ads. I don't care who it is.
5. That time you had sex with a model from one of them.
6. The Delta Sky Club lounge at JFK.
7. Wireless vacuum cleaners.
8. Flowers that look like they were drawn by Dr. Seuss.
9. Wearing a brand-new outfit for the very first time.
10. Knowing that if all else fails, you can always go to the New York Public Library for the Performing Arts and watch a professionally filmed capture of the original cast of *August: Osage County*.

# Looking for Generous

He was a regular, he was kinda hot, and he was an investment banker. Or rather, in my mind he was an investment banker. I had no idea what this man did for a living, or what his name was for that matter, but he was always freshly home from work in an expensive-looking suit when I'd arrive. And investment banker was the main type of job I imagined for a person who had to wear a suit. Sure, there are plenty of jobs that require a person to wear a suit, but I would have been hard-pressed to name more than three (beyond funeral attendant, lawyer, and actor playing a lawyer on TV). At the time, my twenty-year-old self had a flimsy job history and little knowledge of working life besides, of course, the one that employed me at the time: having sex for money.

As this gay Gordon Gekko and I traded our assets of bodily fluids, I glanced over at the polished mid-century modern mahogany desk piled with important-looking documents and spotted a copy of that week's *TimeOut New York*, opened to the LGBT section. There, smack-dab in the middle of the page amid listings of drag shows and circuit parties, was a large picture of me and my best friend advertising the show we would be performing at Joe's Pub that night. The john, who really did look like a poor man's Michael Douglas in his *Wall Street* era, noticed me staring at it . . . but neither of us acknowledged it. Besides the embarrassment for us both, we were busy: the stock market was open, and he was IP-ing my O.

Between the ages of twenty and twenty-three, I supported myself by hooking up with cash-wielding strangers I met on Craigslist all over New York City and, on a few particularly desperate and Mann Act–defying days of the month, New Jersey. Sex work obviously isn't anything new, and if I had a nickel for every gay guy I know who sold some part of his body as a broke twentysomething, I'd have enough money to hire twenty sex workers of my own. One wrinkle in the midst of my tenure in the oldest profession that made my experience unique, however, was that while I was a sex worker, I was also on television.

"On television" is a generous term, but technically it was true. It's not like I was starring on *Murphy Brown* circa 1991 (God, how I wish). Instead I was on the wildly unpopular gay cable network called Logo doing our show *Jeffery and Cole Casserole*, for which we were being paid historically little.

The original idea for my new day job came to me when I was on the train home from a trip to Fire Island. Not only had I had a Herculean amount of anonymous sex, including a memorable experience atop the steering wheel of one of those giant Bobcat machines someone had left on the beach, but I'd spent the remaining crumbs of my checking account on an overpriced drink (or twelve) that I was too young to have legally ordered in the first place. I was sitting in the train car watching Long Island pass by, getting closer and closer to the city I couldn't afford to be living in. While I should have been wondering how the hell I'd pay my rent the following week, I was as usual ignoring the problem and flipping through the pages of the beach read I'd never once opened during my trip. The train was crammed with the usual crowd of brain-fried and bloodshot-eyed gay men returning home like soldiers from a Speedo-clad war of muscles and narcotics. There happened to be two boys around my age across the aisle from me who were cute enough for me to be eavesdropping on their conversation.

One of them was telling the other about how he'd been making money by posting ads on Craigslist's "Men Seeking Men" section and indicating that he was "looking for generous." Apparently, there were all these rich men on Craigslist who would click on the profile of a "generous seeker" and pay them to hook up. Seeing as the number of online hookups I was having at the time could have been submitted to Guinness World Records, I figured, *Why not starting charging for admission?* The boy telling the story was cute but not much cuter than I was, plus in comparison to my twenty-year-old self he was basically ancient, by which I mean twenty-six at most.

Not even two hours after the train had pulled into Penn Station, I had rushed home, posted an ad, gone to an apartment on the

Upper West Side, and was one hundred dollars closer to paying that month's rent.

My first time was with a bald man in his midforties who told me he was a news producer for a popular cable network. He seemed exhausted and like he had just been smoking crystal meth. Both things were undoubtedly true. The whole thing must have lasted no more than half an hour, as quick and clinical as getting a flu shot, with none of the side effects. That is . . . if your flu shot was being administered by a soporific man in ratty-looking gym shorts and flip-flops with hard-core porn playing on a TV in the corner. We lay down on his unmade bed with sheets reeking of the unslept and started to simply jerk off next to each other. His phone kept ringing and beeping with text notifications the whole time before he eventually got up, stormed across the room, shut off his phone, slammed it down in frustration, and shouted, "I fucking hate election years!"

Mere minutes later I finished, and the mere visual of my doing so was enough for him to follow suit before he sent me on my way without my ever once having to so much as touch him. Nothing about that first experience was difficult. It didn't feel seedy or immoral or wrong. In fact, it was a little disappointing. I'd psyched myself up into thinking what I was doing was so punk, so rock-and-roll, so shocking that by the time I finished, I would be such a new, more badass version of myself that people wouldn't even recognize me. However, as I walked back home past Lincoln Center, my dried cum gluing my American Apparel V-neck T-shirt to my stomach, I thought, *Is that all there is?*

The eventual answer: no, Peggy Lee, it isn't.

I dove headfirst into this new day job for which I suspected I might actually be skilled. Nearly everyone who hired me was nice enough and as respectful as you can be when you're naked and erect with a stranger. There was a friendly man who owned a dance shoe store in a sleepy part of Brooklyn, who would hire me to come over after closing. The store lights would be out, and the metal security gate would be pulled down with just enough room for me to crawl underneath it. Once inside the cramped store, surrounded by leotards and Capezio tap shoes, we would hook up on one of those short, old-fashioned stools with the built-in device to measure your foot while I stared at a poster of a male ballerina jetéing at the bar, the paper yellowing with age but the man's face as handsome as the day it was taped to the water-stained wall.

There was a doctor who smelled distinctly like the onions at Subway who only wanted to blindfold me and give me a blow job. He lived in an upscale high rise, and one time I saw a very well-known movie star in the lobby getting his mail, so every time I went over I would fantasize that I was actually there to meet the movie star instead. I still can't watch that actor's movies without thinking about the onions at Subway.

Another man lived in a dollhouse-size West Village studio containing more potted plants than I have ever seen in my life. It was like being paid to have sex with Audrey II from *Little Shop of Horrors*, endlessly being poked and prodded by vines and branches in one or both of our orifices.

There was the guy who always insisted I come over wearing sunscreen, no matter the weather. I would lather myself in SPF 50 in the freezing dead of a January night before heading to the Upper East Side, where he'd spend the entire hour smelling every inch of my melanoma-resistant body while murmuring things like "Is it safe to swim, lifeguard?" under his stale breath.

Another john, the Big Baby, as I used to refer to him to friends, definitely earned his moniker. This fifty-something-year-old man would open the door with the saddest of puppy dog eyes and apologize for being bad before I even walked in the door. I didn't really have to do anything besides pinch his nipples and watch as he wiggled around and pouted. I suppose that describes a lot of people's marriages.

There was a swollen man who paid me to come over twice a week and rub lotion on his equally swollen ankles. He had some sort of horrible condition that made them super dry and flaky, but he was too big to reach them. He was a writer, and his dusty bookshelves were full of the type of vintage gay fiction I was just beginning to discover, so we had a lot in common to talk about. We never went too deep, sticking mostly to the topics of Edmund White novels and my dick, but mostly the focus remained on his ankles. However, one snowy winter day I allowed a bit of reality into the equation when I showed up in the decomposing Converse I wore daily, and he asked why I wasn't wearing proper snow boots. I admitted I didn't have any, and before I could even get the lotion onto his ankles, we were in a cab going to a shoe store (not the one I sometimes hooked up in—we weren't shopping for ballet slippers!), where he bought me a pair of waterproof boots I still have to this very day. The only problem was that I then felt obligated to wear them every time I went over to his apartment, no matter the weather—like the way you continue to wear the hideous sweater your aunt gave you for your birthday every time you see her until you outgrow it or she dies.

A lot of these guys became regulars that I grew to depend on and who were always there for me when I was in the most desperate of binds. Like Paul. Paul had a micropenis and was very insecure about it, so all he ever wanted to do was pleasure me. This must have been exactly what George Gershwin was thinking when he wrote about "nice work if you can get it."

Paul was extremely kind, tender, and caring. He was the type of john who I would contact before he ever reached out to me because I knew how reliable his hundred dollars were. I'd send texts like "Hey hey. Wanna get together today?"—which he clearly knew meant "Hi, please give me money," but he never batted an eye and always helped, no questions asked.

After nearly a year of seeing Paul, it was suddenly Christmastime, and I was set to fly home to celebrate. However, I had put off coming up with that month's $750 rent, and I was way past my landlord's third warning. I couldn't leave town with the prospect of returning to an eviction looming over my holidays like some terrible strain of mistletoe. The week had been slow, with so many of my usual customers spending their money on the holidays instead of, well, me. So I had twenty-four hours to come up with my rent. With a freezing day of having to find at least four gigs by nighttime ahead of me, I woke up scrambling.

It was a Saturday morning, and very few people were replying to my ad. I deleted it a few times, reposting with a hopefully more enticing photo, but nothing was happening. There were a few replies, but they either ghosted or wanted to schedule for the next week. My already high anxiety was climbing to heights taller than the Rockefeller tree twinkling across town. I thought about texting always-dependable Paul, but I'd done that exact thing the previous Saturday and then blown the money on a cardigan to wear while performing in a Christmas show at the Midtown Ars Nova theater. I wrestled with biting the bullet and just doing it again and risking an overstep. However, I feared I would officially alienate Paul from my future.

But as is often the case in my life, desperation got the better of me, and I decided that if texting Paul again was the straw that broke the camel's back of my reliance on him, well, then . . . bring on the camel. I had rent to pay.

I texted Paul a completely honest request: "Hey Paul. Do you happen to be around today? I'm trying to come up with some money before I leave tomorrow for the holidays. I'll do whatever you want. Lemme know."

Paul told me to come over right away, and I wasted no time. I arrived to his usual warm smile with Whitney Houston's Christmas album playing just loud enough to hear. In the corner of his living room stood a beautiful live Christmas tree, complete with its festive pine aroma, and it dawned on me that this would be the first time I'd ever had sex for money in a place decorated for the holidays. Suddenly, I was surprised to be hit by an enormous melancholic wave I hadn't seen coming. I love Christmas, and something about bringing it into what I was doing made the thing I was doing feel strange for the very first time.

I reckon it was the impending pressure of going home. When I went home, I felt like I had something to prove. I had to make my life sound as fabulous and enviable as possible because otherwise I was just a college dropout wasting my early twenties making stupid videos for no money. No one was putting that pressure on me but myself, but I was doing enough heavy lifting for everybody.

In a lot of ways, my life at the time was an enviable and exciting thing. I was making things, people were seeing the things and even writing articles about the things. I really was a working artist. I just didn't make any money from that work. Instead, I couldn't afford my rent, and I was about to do whatever I had to do to this man's micropenis while Whitney Houston heralded the first Noel in the background.

"Jeff, everything okay?" Paul asked with genuine concern as I stared sadly at his Christmas tree, wondering about the origins of one ornament and then the next.

"Yeah. Fine. I'm fine," I said, snapping back to the job at hand, flashing my best fake smile. I never wanted my johns to see me sad—I never wanted my johns to see me at all.

Paul and I went to his bedroom and repeated our usual soulless routine together. When we'd finish, he'd always go get a towel before cleaning me off, sheepishly staring at the wall or anywhere other than me. The job over and the moment passed. But this time, when he returned with the towel, he looked me directly in the eye.

"I just want you to know I am really grateful for these times we have together." Paul's words were quiet and mannered. "I know doing what you do has got to take a toll on you."

"Naw!" I said, performing the perky, positive-minded twink he was paying for. "I like it!"

He looked at me with a tender frown, his and my own silence drowning out the holiday musical reverie still floating through the speakers in the other room. In his sympathetic stare I could see him taking in my pain and anxiety, which I thought I had hidden so well. After a moment he simply nodded and added, "Well, either way. Merry Christmas."

He then counted out ten crisp one-hundred-dollar bills across my bare stomach. I lay there, motionless, naked, and staring at this money, which would solve all my problems. In one incredibly generous move this man, who knew so little about me, besides the shape of my penis, had solved the entire problem that was my day. And without seeing it coming, I burst into tears.

He grabbed me, pulling me into a tight embrace I didn't know I so desperately needed. We had never hugged before, and we never hugged again after, but in that moment, the glow of his Christmas tree lighting the living room outside the door like it does when you're a kid counting down to morning on Christmas Eve, he held me in his arms as my shoulders loosened for the first time all day with the sensation of a saved Christmas.

......

Sometimes it wasn't as Norman Rockwell meets *Midnight Cowboy* as these encounters might suggest. Sometimes the worst of an already trying day job presented the types of problems you might picture. There was the obvious: body odor, shortchanging me, constant cancellations, treating me like a whore . . . which, granted, I was. There were also men like the guy who could only cum if he slapped my face really hard, a cornucopia of crack addicts, and the guy who always wore so much concealer that afterward my clothes looked like I'd been in a street fight with Tammy Faye Bakker.

There was a man who hired me to come over early one Sunday morning and have sex with another guy while his wife was out shopping. The idea was that he'd just sit and watch us have sex, which he did, quite happily. Speaking of happy, the minute I arrived and spotted the sex worker who'd be my morning scene partner, I thought to myself, *Well, I could get used to THIS*. The fun faded when, midway through the hookup, we heard the front door open. The john's face turned so ashen white it looked as though he'd eaten raw oysters at Applebee's. In his panic, he furiously pointed at his walk-in closet, where the other sex worker and I scurried our slick nude bodies like characters in a Joe Orton farce. While we hid inside the closet, our eyes met, and unable to help it, we started making out again, which was really hot until the john flung the door open and angrily demanded we get the fuck out. He'd sent his wife downstairs on some fool's errand. As I made my escape out of the apartment, I noticed a framed show poster for Betty Buckley in *Sunset Boulevard* in their foyer . . . and I thought, *Oh, sweetie, your wife knows*.

There was an out-of-towner who would come to New York and book a room at a fancy hotel. I would meet him in the lobby bar, where he'd slip me his hotel room key so I could go up to his room and tie myself to the bed with pieces of bedsheets he'd ripped up. Clearly this was a man who laughed at the term "security deposit." Tying yourself spread-eagle to an unfamiliar bed is a tricky endeavor, especially when you're approaching it with the enthusiasm of a doorstop. I wasn't stupid enough to get myself fully bound into helplessness. Once he returned to the room, I'd be blindfolded just enough that he could live his fantasy while I kept an eye toward the exit in case I needed it. Then he'd bite me all over my body while pleasuring himself. I saw this guy quite a few times at various five-star hotels around town until the day he bit my ankle so hard it drew blood, and I thought, *Maybe I should be charging more?*

There was the time I had spent a weekend turning tricks before I was scheduled to film a guest appearance on *30 Rock* as Liz Lemon's cousin Randy, who comes to New York City for a wild gay weekend. At one point in the episode, Liz comes in to discover Randy waking up on the sofa with "SLUT" written across his forehead. What the audience didn't know was that I had gotten full-blown gonorrhea from a client, so I spent every moment of downtime sneaking off to my dressing room to change underwear to avoid staining a sofa on NBC. That said, I was able to cross one item off my bucket list: "Film my first television appearance across from Tina Fey and James Franco, while having a leaking penis."

There were also the *constant* cancellations. Sometimes they occurred far enough in advance that I didn't have to waste my time and hot water on a shower, but sometimes the johns bailed infuriatingly last-minute, like the time I'd spent all day messaging back and forth with a man who lived in a doorman building on the Upper East Side. When we'd finally made arrangements after the type of correspondence involved in planning a Supreme Court hearing, I arrived at his building and asked for apartment 4B, only to discover that he'd turned off his phone. When even his doorman couldn't get him to answer, I was seething so intensely that I ripped a page out of the Moleskine journal in my backpack and wrote in big block letters "WATCH YOUR BACK 4B" and handed it to the doorman before leaving and texting the guy that my pimp would find him when he least expected it and that if I were him, I would stop leaving the house. Manic behavior? Sure. Fun? You betcha!

One particularly lonely and desperate day, I showed up at the apartment building of a man who I should have known would be trouble based solely on the fact that he asked for too many photos. I sent three, but he asked for five before he started getting specific. He wanted me to send a photo of my ass from the side, then up in the air, then from the other side. This was especially uneventful given that my ass has always had the girth and overall presence of a yoga mat someone drove a tractor over. He wanted to see me from so many angles it felt less like he was offering to pay me one hundred dollars for a blow job and more that he planned on flipping me into a two-family duplex.

Finally, when I went over, he insisted on meeting me outside. As I walked up, he looked me up and down like the comic book asshole that he was and said, "I'm not paying for that." With my usual lack of self-control, I instinctively punched the Starbucks cup he was holding out of his hand and screamed at the top of my lungs: "FUCK YOU AND PAY ME FOR MY DICK, YOU ASSHOLE!" He didn't . . . and frankly, that's on me: it was my asshole he was supposed to have paid for, not my dick. Apples and oranges.

During this time, I didn't date, and for the most part I pretty much stopped having any sex for pleasure. Sure, I obsessively pined after cute boys, but the idea of going on a date and getting to know someone felt too scary. I liked the successful version of myself I believed I was putting out into the world and shuddered at the idea of anyone glimpsing down the creaky old stairs into the dirt floor basement piled with boxes of scratched records and dusty keepsakes that was my actual self-confidence.

There were a few detours into sparks of romance that I'd inevitably extinguish. I met a very cute guy, Justin, online who had just moved to town from Florida. We started these flirtatious Facebook chats that grew and grew in frequency, with the type of fortitude one only finds behind a profile pic. Sometimes we'd even plan to hang out, but I'd always find a way to chicken out and pretend to be sick or out of town or busy with an important work deadline that didn't exist. But the real reason was always the same: I was embarrassed to tell a stranger about the way I made money.

Meanwhile, prospects were improving for my and Cole's careers in the downtown queer performance scene, and by "improving" I mean we were booked to do a one-night show in an art space in Soho. This particular venue required you to pay a flat fee (which you'd ideally recoup in ticket sales) and pay their lighting and sound technician to run your show. This would have been totally fine if we hadn't been a tad over exposed at this point and afraid to charge twenty bucks a ticket. Instead, we had given friends and acquaintances free tickets in a desperate attempt to avoid having to perform to no one. Needless to say, we had to come up with a lump of money by the time we showed up to tech rehearsal, and I'd, of course, waited until the very last minute to do so.

I awoke that morning with both preshow jitters and the ever-familiar money dread that colored my daily life. Our show, *A Conversation about Annie Potts*, was at eight that night, and tech rehearsal was at three, which meant I had to come up with the cash in the short window between waking up and getting down-town to the venue.

Our show had absolutely NOTHING to do with the actress Annie Potts, by the way. We'd picked the title in some drunken mad dash to get the information to the venue a few weeks prior with the notion that we'd surely come up with something brilliant, but if the shit hit the fan we could always just sit down and discuss how much we liked Annie Potts. I have absolutely no recollection of what the show was about, and neither does Cole; the script was lost to some defunct email address from long ago. All I can remember is that, due to the title, we added a beat at the very end of the show where we turned to the audience and said in unison, "And this has been a conversation about Annie Potts," which was followed by a blackout and bewildered applause.

But as the great P. T. Barnum never said, "In order to get to opening night, you have to suck off some strangers for money first."

Like that weekend before Christmas with Paul, I lined up another triple-header of gigs, setting a record for myself. Two were regulars, neither one interesting enough to mention here except for the fact that one of them would not stop bragging about how the last prostitute he'd hired had once (allegedly) worked for Kevin Spacey. I don't know about you, but having to chat about your (alleged) six degrees of Kevin Spacey on the twink sex worker scale when you've got a show to tech is my definition of tedious.

What the first two gigs lacked in memorability, the third more than made up for. His name was Richard, and he'd continue to be memorable for the next six months. Richard wasn't really his name, but I'm calling him that because (a) I don't want to be sued, and (b) he had the distinct look of a Richard. But then again, don't all gay men of a certain age? Almost all gay men go from looking like a Zak to someday waking up as a Richard. Those are just the rules.

It was around eleven that morning when I arrived at Richard's brick prewar building in Murray Hill for the first time.

"Hi. I'm here for Rich—" I began to say to the doorman before he cut me off.

"Richard in 12C?" He'd clearly seen one thousand others like me before.

I said yes, and he pointed me toward the old, rickety elevator in the corner of the room, where an elderly operator stood awaiting his next passenger. Elevator rides with elevator operators were an especially off-putting part of my job. As if the brief exchange with the doorman isn't intimately nerve-racking enough, suddenly you find yourself locked in a tiny ascending room alone with a strange old man on your way to enter a larger stationary room with an older and stranger man.

I made my way to Richard's door at the end of the long, tiled hallway, which was lit by stained glass sconces and smelled like old New York money. Before I could even knock, the door flung open, and there was Richard.

He stood in a white terry cloth robe that was too short for his very long, slippery frame. His shaky posture was arched and crooked, like an Ikea bookshelf that's been put together while you're on edibles. His body was quite thin and gaunt and sported a pronounced paunch that simply screamed bourbon. Or, at the very least, rye.

The robe itself had been stolen from whatever fabulous hotel's logo was still barely stitched on its breast pocket. It was frayed, worn, and slightly discolored, all traces of glamour faded in the wash many years ago, but with the ghost of it all remaining. His face was similar, a reflection of something that had once been handsome and striking. He had a statuesque jawline and a strong nose covered in "gin blossoms," all still visible beneath the wear and tear of many years and fewer washes. His piercing blue irises were surrounded by a redness winning a battle with the whites of his eyes, giving them a patriotic American flag motif.

"Jeff?" he asked urgently and loudly, his voice echoing through the empty hallway.

As my life as a sex worker progressed, I had started to go by Jeff instead of Jeffery while I was on the clock. I never really thought about it at the time, but I suppose it had something to do with the fact that nobody in my real life had ever called me Jeff, so it felt like I was playing a character.

I had also taken to claiming to be a sophomore dance student at Juilliard. Thinking back on this, it's utterly wild to me that I never considered that I did not, in any way, have the body of a dance student. While I was very thin, you couldn't have found a defined or engaged muscle on my body with a magnifying glass. I really enjoyed pretending to be a dancer, though. It's a beautiful art that I claimed to take very seriously. I'd gab on and on about some hilarious recent story that had happened at school. "The craziest thing happened to my friend Lisa during floor work last week. She pulled her meniscus doing a heel clack!" No john ever called me out on these obvious fabrications, but I suppose fantasy is a two-way street.

"Yep. I'm Jeff. And you're Richard?" I asked, but he'd already turned to grandly bounce back inside like Auntie Mame, gesturing me to follow.

"Oh, I'm *so* thrilled you're here!" he called out over his shoulder, stepping into his sunken living room and making his way to the well-stocked bar beneath a ceiling-high window overlooking Third Avenue.

The apartment was fabulous. Old New York architecture, with big ornate arches, windows everywhere and sunlight spilling across the gleaming hardwood floors, and French doors leading to a wraparound terrace.

"Can I get you anything? Scotch?" Richard asked, fidgeting with a glass like a person with ants in his pants. Except, of course, he wasn't wearing any.

The clock on the wall, next to a casually hung original Andy

Warhol portrait of Richard himself, reminded me it was just past 11:00 a.m.

"I'm good!" I chirped.

His own glass clinking with melting ice cubes and top-shelf booze, he ushered me into the kitchen, where I saw an enormous pile of twenties beside an equally enormous pile of cocaine.

"How much was it you said in the ad? I forget," he asked, snorting a quick line, then counting out some of the twenties.

"One hundred," I told him.

He turned, with a big cocaine grin and outer space eyes, then pressed the wad of cash into my hand.

"I'm *so* thrilled you're here, Jeff! Really, I am!" He sang it out to the ceiling like it was an audience of exposed beams.

His energy was manic, needy, chaotic, but also oddly assured. A Looney Tunes cartoon character on Viagra. He was the kind of person who could spontaneously quote Nietzsche or rip the ring out of a hand grenade with his teeth, and you wouldn't be surprised by either. Which is to say that there was something truly special about him.

"And you go to Juilliard?! WOW! JUST WOW!"

"I do! Sophomore," I told him with the utterly false confidence that always felt good to try on for size.

"I've been friends with *many* a Juilliard survivor in my time!" he said with a knowing wink from his red, white, and blue eyes. "That place is a real bitch, but worth it, huh?"

I nodded as he snorted another line, then snapping to attention, he looked at me like we were two highly professional colleagues in a corporate room cutting the crap and getting into a negotiation.

"Okay, Jeff, how much do I owe you?" he asked.

"One hundred, but you just—"

He had already turned around and was counting out the bills. He would have made both the worst and best bank teller in the history of the world, depending on which side of the counter you stood on.

"Jeff, I've been up for the past twenty-four hours," he said calmly, like saying, "Jeff, I'm a Libra." I bet he was a Libra, by the way.

As he counted the money, taking breaks to pick up his drink, his hand shook briefly like a maraca before he snorted a line of coke and slowed down. He rambled on about his previous night's escapades at an art function for an institution whose board he served on. He bragged a lot about a friendship with someone who was somehow affiliated with Mary-Kate Olsen, but he kept insisting, "To be clear, I don't know either her *or* her sister," as if it were something I might have judged him for. On the list of things I was judging, however, knowing a former *Full House* cast member would not have been included.

In between his anecdotes, he continued to hand me more and more cash, each time with no recollection of the last, possessed by the ghost of an ATM. Of course I shoved it all in my pockets without mentioning a thing. Anything else would have been rude, and I may be a lot of things, but rude to my elders is not one of them.

Pretty soon he led me to his bedroom. As we passed through his art-filled hallway, he pointed out the names of various famous painters and photographers I was too naive to have ever heard of. As soon as we entered his bedroom, we collapsed onto his bed for the whole reason I was there in the first place.

Throughout the encounter, he continued to snort lines of coke off the nightstand, while I wondered if a nightstand is still a nightstand when it's 11:30 a.m. and it's covered with cocaine. We made out, his breath the smell of a *Saturday Night Live* after-party in 1976, while we jerked off next to each other. Remarkably, he finished before I did, then stood up over me.

"I want to watch you," he said as he snorted yet another line, watching me jerk off with gleeful focus. That's when I noticed a small red dot forming just below his nostril, like an impoverished little ladybug who had sold her spots and found herself bare and clinging to a strand of narcotic-covered nose hair.

Now, if you ever find yourself lying naked before a stranger who has a small (but growing!) bead of blood hanging off his nostril, and this stranger is paying you to jerk off beneath him, and you've got a tech rehearsal to get to . . . my first piece of advice is to check in with your body. Is your head and, most specifically, mouth far enough away that in the event that this droplet of blood rains down it will land, ideally, not on your face or mouth?

Fortunately, I was well positioned, with my head far enough away from any potential splatter. He was breathing heavily, worked up from his recent orgasm and the mountains of cocaine fueling his arteries. I was in a mad dash to make myself finish, conjuring every dependable image in my spank bank. With each of his heavy breaths, the bead of blood jiggled and loosened from the grip of his nose hair. I thought of stopping and telling him to please, for the love of God, get a tissue, but that just would've slowed things down, and I was far too interested in getting out of there as quickly as humanly possible.

The blood droplet grew bigger, and all weather forecasts were pointing to it crashing down any minute. My mind was somewhere else, fantasizing about something sexy like a shirtless Cheyenne Jackson mowing a lawn or David Sedaris saying something nice about me, as I neared my way to glory. I began writhing about as if I were in utter ecstasy, but really I was just angling myself further away from the impending bloodbath from my coked-up first-time buyer. Suddenly, yet inevitably if you believe in gravity, the bead of blood became dislodged from its resting position, and I watched as it came crashing down in slow motion. I really revved up my writhing, attempting to make my way off the bed entirely, but it was quite simply too late, and I quite simply had too many limbs. The blood droplet came crashing onto my thigh just as I climaxed, my cum meeting and mixing with his blood the way some people mix ketchup and mustard. I lay there, covered in the perfect sauce to serve a perverted vampire while I waited for him to get me a towel.

As I was on my way out the door post-shower, he asked me one last time, "Jeff, how much was it that I owe you?"

This time I felt I'd more than earned the extra.

"Two hundred," I said.

Then I left, paid for that night's venue, did the tech rehearsal, did the show, and for that glorious hour in front of the audience it was as if I hadn't had a stranger's cokey blood on my body that morning at all.

......

I continued seeing Richard on a fairly regular basis for the next several months. The situation was usually the same: an odd time of day, cocaine, jittery conversation about the previous night's party with some trendy-sounding art person in attendance. He was always aggressively generous and kind, with a merriment about him that was impossible not to be charmed by.

When he wasn't in his tattered robe, he always wore the same thing: his eccentric little uniform. No matter the time of year or time of day, he wore a vintage Vivienne Westwood seersucker suit. And literally every single time, he would always find a way to bring the conversation back to the story of how he had found the suit in Paris many years before. He claimed that he was reaching for it in a vintage boutique in Paris, and as he did so he turned to see another hand reaching for it at the exact same time. When he looked up and discovered it was none other than Vivienne Westwood herself, he snatched the suit and hissed, "Finders keepers, bitch," to her surprised amusement. It's hard to believe that story for many reasons, the main one being why would she need to buy her own suit and the other being that it was told by Richard. But I never once stopped him from telling it all over again.

He continued to be genuinely interested in hearing about me and my life, which was tricky since my entire persona with him had been a lie. There are only so many stories you can tell about being a dance student when you're not a dance student. So I started attempting to phase out the Juilliard storyline. I was proud of everything happening with my comedy career, and one day I built up the courage to confess to him that I'd dropped out of Juilliard to pursue my true love: comedy.

"That's beautiful, Jeff! What is comedy if not a dance of laughter?" he theorized in a scholarly fashion between sips and snuffs of breakfast gin and weekday cocaine.

I told him about my projects with Cole: the videos and the shows around town. He was intrigued and impressed. Richard was the first person in this part of my life for whom I had intentionally pulled back the curtain separating the safety net of fiction and the reality of a nascent career. I had been working really hard to create two personas at once: the quick-witted Jeffery that I played in daily life and the sexy, confident young twink people expected when they hired Jeff. As I opened up about my creative endeavors to Richard, I felt Jeff and Jeffery come together as one, letting some air out of the tire of shame that I was never not carrying around on my neck.

A few days later, Richard called me at the crack of dawn (or, in Richard's world, happy hour).

"Jeff! I watched the videos!" he shouted the second I answered. I was groggy, and it took me a second to realize what he meant.

"Good morning. Oh, that's so nice of you to say—"

He continued to talk over me, our conversations always his monologue.

"I was sitting here watching your videos, and suddenly it hit me!" his tone shifted to grave seriousness, as if the future of mankind depended on what he'd say next. "Have you ever seen Jerry Lewis in *Cinderfella*?"

"I don't think I have," I said.

"Here's what we should do," he instructed. "You and your tiny friend from the videos [he meant Cole] need to come over. I'll show you my favorite scene from *Cinderfella*, and then I'll take you two out to a fabulous dinner. All on me! And don't worry. Just dinner, no funny business! Well, besides Jerry, of course!" He cackled at himself. "How's tomorrow night?!"

Cole was in. As they have said before in interviews, Cole was also doing sex work at this time. It made for a very "Mickey and Judy putting on a show" meets *My Own Private Idaho*–type existence between us. We'd get together and exchange the tales of our respective days, like old war buddies reminiscing about 'Nam. We even had a little bit of overlap, sharing a few johns who had no idea we were connected to one another, let alone a burgeoning comedy duo.

I didn't realize it at the time, but we were following in a long line of other budding artists trying to make their way in the city while supporting themselves through sex work. In fact, many of the people Richard had known in Warhol's factory probably had similar experiences. The story of selling sex as a means of survival while pursuing a creative path was and remains as old as the dilapidated laundromat I lived above. There was something I found comforting about feeling a part of a long-trodden tradition, even in the darkest moments of it all. I felt the echo of sex worker–artists who had come before me (no pun intended), and I felt proud to be part of this complicated fraternity.

Cole and I got together before we went over for Richard's movie night and had a few drinks to grease the wheels of what was sure to be a Nascar Daytona 400–level ride of a night. We were sufficiently buzzed by the time we arrived and rode the elevator up to Richard's apartment, the usual operator giving us a look that said, *Oh god, now he's got two of them?*

If we were buzzed when we arrived, Richard was tanked.

"Well, well, well . . . look who's here!" Richard slurred as if he hadn't invited us over in the first place. "What can I get you boys to drink?"

Without even closing his own front door behind us, Richard was already slinking over to his bar and pouring us whiskey. I closed the door for him and eagerly took the cocktail. It was freezing out, yet he was still wearing that Vivienne Westwood seersucker suit with loafers and no socks. He looked ready for Easter in the Hamptons while Cole and I looked ready to hit the slopes.

We sat, enjoying our drinks, while Richard showered us with praise for our videos. This was, of course, a welcome change from my first visit when the only thing he showered me with was his cocaine nosebleed.

"Our reservation is in half an hour, so we don't have much time, but I have to show you some of *Cinderfella*!"

The movie was already cued up on the TV, paused on one of Richard's favorite bits. He pressed PLAY. *Cinderfella* follows the basic plot points of the Cinderella story, putting Jerry Lewis in the lead as a goofy man who dreams of finding his father's fortune and a happier life. Eventually, he is turned into a suave prince and attends a ball. The scene Richard wanted to show us was of Jerry making his entrance down a grand staircase to the rousing music of Count Basie's orchestra. He goes into a big comedic dance that is pure Jerry Lewis brilliance as Richard ecstatically pointed out every minute detail.

It was a great scene, but I was incredibly hungry. When it was already nearing the time of our dinner reservation and we were onto Richard's third favorite *Cinderfella* scene, I was getting antsy. By the time we left, we were well past half an hour late for the reservation, with all three of us shit-faced on whiskey and Jerry Lewis trivia.

On our way out into the cold night, Richard wrapped himself in an elaborate velvet opera cape he had recently purchased in Chile. With the enormous black cape, the seersucker suit, his towering frame, and his bloodshot eyes, he looked like Count Dracula at the Kentucky Derby.

As we made our way down the street, people passing by stopped to look quizzically at Richard's outfit. Then, just as we were almost to the restaurant, Richard tripped over his long cape and tumbled headfirst onto the icy sidewalk.

It was incredibly jarring, but Richard wasn't fazed. He let out a little groan, got up, and dusted himself off. Maybe it was the liquid courage or maybe just the sheer confidence one feels when wearing a Chilean opera cape, but either way, he didn't notice the small cut on his forehead that was now leaking blood onto his face.

"Are you all right?" I asked, pointing out the gash.

He shrugged.

"I'm fine. We're only a block away. I'll just handle it there," he said, resuming his confident strut to our destination.

We finally arrived at the swanky restaurant an hour past our reservation. As we made our way inside, a woman brushed past us, glancing over at Richard's bleeding forehead and gonzo outfit in muted shock. Richard turned to us and whispered so loudly that they could have heard it in Connecticut, "That was Maria Shriver!" Cole and I looked back at the woman who was most definitely not Maria Shriver and said something like, "Wow. Very cool."

The restaurant staff wasn't fazed by our tardiness or by Richard's bleeding forehead. In fact, the entire staff reacted to his charming belligerence in a way that told us he came here often. They even knew him by name.

"This way to your table, Richard. And I'll get you some napkins as well," the seen-it-all-before hostess told us as she directed us to our table before bringing Richard a stack of paper cocktail napkins for his forehead.

Richard got his forehead taken care of, and we ordered lots of wine and lots of food and continued to talk about *Cinderfella* and who can remember what else? It must have been interesting enough because we closed the place down. Sometime very late that night, after I'd said goodbye to Cole, I boarded the subway home and made my way back to my apartment, all the while drunkenly wondering, *What the fuck is it with this guy and blood?*

......

The last time I ever saw Richard was on a spring day a few months after the Jerry Lewis dinner. I'd seen him a few times in the weeks prior, and it was clear then that his partying had gotten even more out of hand. There were more cuts, bruises, and other signs of the wear and tear of a long life of hard living. He was like one of the old paintings that hung on his wall, but one that looked more and more like it had just come out of a badly driven moving van. One day he invited me to see *Exit the King* on Broadway, which was playing a few blocks from my apartment. It starred Geoffrey Rush, Susan Sarandon, and Andrea Martin. I was excited to see it and even more so that he'd booked us a table at Joe Allen's before the show.

I arrived in front of the theater to meet him at the box office to get the tickets then go to dinner. When I got there, he was standing alone on the sidewalk in his seersucker suit like always, but now looking worse than ever. The bloodshot eyes were even redder, with a yellow hew where the whites had once been. His skin was sickly pale, nearly as white as his cocaine mountains, and he was trembling underneath the opera cape, which that day's warm weather rendered even more ridiculous. If he'd looked like Dracula before, now he was looking more like death itself.

"Richard? Are you all right?" I asked, approaching him carefully. He looked so weak I feared he could be knocked over by words alone. He was cowering against the walls of the theater, the building itself being the only thing holding him up.

"Jeff, I can't join you for the show and dinner tonight," he stuttered in a monotone he'd never used before, staring at the sidewalk, all traces of his eccentric persona gone.

His trembling fingers shoved an envelope containing the tickets into my hands along with a thick wad of cash, wet from his clammy sweat.

"I want you to go and have dinner before the show. Bring somebody. Maybe a date? There's enough in there for Joe Allen's or wherever you want to eat." He began to cry. "I don't think you'll be seeing me for a while. I am going to get some help. But take care, Jeff, and keep at it, okay?"

I stood there unsure what to say, and he did the same until finally he wiped a tear from his eye, dejectedly patted me on the shoulder, and began to limp away, his entire person an empty bottle of scotch that had once been full and expensive.

"Thank you," I said.

He smiled back at me.

"Thank you, Jeff."

I never heard from him again.

I walked the few blocks back home, where I opened my laptop in bed to kill time on Facebook, now with an hour until a show to which I had great seats but no one to go with. Cole and other friends were busy, so I thought about selling the tickets outside the theater to pocket the money along with the wad of cash he'd given me for dinner. But I also really wanted to see the play.

On my AIM chat, I noticed that Justin, the cute guy who I'd flaked on time and time again, was online. We hadn't chatted in a while, since one particularly last-minute cancellation too many on my part. At this point, I couldn't remember the last actual date I'd been on.

I took a deep breath and nervously typed a message.

"Hey."

"Hey," he replied immediately.

I swallowed the shame that was freezing my fingers into stillness, then continued to type.

"So, this guy I sometimes have sex with for money gave me tickets to *Exit the King* tonight and cash for dinner. He can't go anymore, but the show is in two hours. I know this is weird, but . . . do you want to come with me?"

It was the first time I'd ever told someone who wasn't a very close friend the truth about what I did for money. It felt very scary and weird, and I was already regretting it when he replied:

"Sure! Eight o'clock?"

We went to the play, held hands in the dark, and had a fabulous dinner afterward. We kissed on the sidewalk outside Joe Allen's and even hung out a few more times before I got too possessive and scared him off. But it was the night of the play that, for the first time, I allowed myself to stop compartmentalizing my life. I stopped separating the Jeff that did sex work and the Jeffery that I was trying to market into a career. All of it was me, and it was that evening that I found the courage to show someone who I really was—even the parts I still carried shame about. I don't know if I would have done that without Richard. Or Paul. Or the guy who bought me waterproof boots. Or even the doctor who smelled like the onions at Subway.

Sometimes now, almost two decades later, when I'm walking around New York, I'll pass a building that floods me with memories of a john or a trick that I turned in whatever apartment window I find myself staring up at. I'll stand on the sidewalk, looking into a window where "Jeff" once stood and made his ever-coveted hundred bucks. I can see him straining to carry his suitcases of worry up to another apartment to make another coin to put in his piggy bank of shame. And I can see him leaving again a half hour later, with a pep in his step from being a little bit richer, but with the glassy-eyed worry that he's ruining himself in the process. And I want to rush across traffic to this young version of myself, grab him, and look him directly in the eyes. First, he'll probably be terrified of this older, puffier, thicker walking portrait of Dorian Gray before him, but once he stops screaming at the ghoulish glimpse into his future, I want to hold him and tell him, "This will all be worth it."

# I Think I'm Alone Now

As far as "sad little gay boy" origin stories go, mine was pretty easy. Sure there was bullying, uneducated bias from family and people around me, fear, pain, blah blah blah. But I can guarantee that almost every other "sad little gay boy" origin story was tougher than mine. My story shares one common thing with millions of others, though: when you're growing up gay in a small town in the late nineties and early two thousands, your brain is wired to think that you're all alone. There are no other little gay boys like you, and as you grow older, you think there are no other teenage boys like you, and when it comes to an adult being like you? You shudder to imagine.

Someday, though, you'll see a nameless flaming florist with three lines on an episode of a popular sitcom, or you'll stumble upon a rainy-day viewing of *The Object of My Affection* on TBS, and you'll unearth a shining glimmer of hope that has been there all along, lurking beneath the shrapnel of your isolation: maybe, just maybe, you are not alone.

By the time I'd hit puberty, attempting to spot or sniff out another gay guy had become, roughly, one trillion percent of my every thought. Anywhere and everywhere—at the mall, the grocery store, in traffic, in the audience of *The Oprah Winfrey Show*.

It was around this time that a friend from school and community theater, Elizabeth, mentioned her boyfriend from church while we snacked on Chick-fil-A on a break from rehearsal for the community theater's production of *Oliver!*

"And he still hasn't kissed me," Elizabeth proclaimed to her audience of fourteen-year-old virgins, as we stuffed our faces with homophobic but delicious French fries without a single thought of caloric intake, the way only fourteen-year-old virgins can.

"Honestly? I think he might be gay," Elizabeth added. At that moment, it was like someone hit the MUTE button. While everyone's mouths continued to speak and chew, the word "gay" sang out all around me like a thousand-person choir echoing in a cathedral of possibility. Elizabeth was no dummy—if she was catching a hint of gay in this guy, then there had to be something to it. She had known I was gay ever since I'd emotionally revealed myself as such in a weighty AIM chat one day after school.

I vowed to myself, right then and there, that I would meet this complete and total stranger who may or may not be gay according to his Backstreet Boys–obsessed girlfriend. And then? Well, duh . . . we would fall into a passionate, all-consuming love affair, and I'd make him mine forever. Elizabeth was super pretty and always dated the cute popular boys, so the way I saw it, this boy she was dating had to be at the very least a seven, and I would've been willing to settle for a four. When her boyfriend showed up to see us on opening night, I was relieved to find that my hunch was correct. With boot-cut jeans fresh off the American Eagle runway (or, at the very least, the outlet mall), sparkling eyes, a crooked grin, and prematurely stubbled face, he was a swaggering, biker jacket–clad James Dean, and suddenly I wanted to be a motorcycle when I grew up.

"Brad's here tonight. Can you believe this will be the first time he's seen me onstage?" Elizabeth asked aghast, like she was Maggie Smith gossiping about a West End theater critic.

"Oh. This is . . . uh . . . Brad . . . the boyfriend, right?" I tried to ask calmly and with nonchalance, like I wasn't some sweaty pervert who had already considered what our last names would sound like when we inevitably combined them to make things easier for Horvath, the son we had adopted from Slovakia after banking our first cool million.

"Yeah. Maybe you can tell me whether or not he's gay," she said as we doused ourselves in Ben Nye "stage dirt" before taking our places for the grisly four-hour sojourn that was this community theater production of Lionel Bart's masterpiece.

The summer 2001 Rome Little Theatre production of *Oliver!* was, in this critic's opinion, one of our community's worst productions of all time. Just close your eyes and imagine northwest Georgians attempting British accents. Picture a set designed by a person who grew up in a cave and had never seen any form of human shelter before. Then, grab a hammer and break the sole air conditioner cooling the cavernous one-hundred-year-old building and settle in for hours in the type of heat you could bake quiche in while you listen to the entire show's score played on the dulcet tones of a Clavinova (look it up). That said, I was absolutely excellent in it.

I played the Artful Dodger, as is required by law for all gay fourteen-year-old boys (look that up too). And to put my own distinctive twist on the role, I insisted on dyeing my hair Lucille Ball red for no apparent reason whatsoever.

My pretty friend Elizabeth played Bet, which, if you ask me, is barely even a role. Other than having a name that conjures Midler or Davis, there's not much to write home about when it comes to Bet. Bet is Nancy's sidekick, Nancy being the raucous alcoholic woman who hangs out with a crew of literal children for some unexplained reason and belts the perfect show tune "As Long as He Needs Me" before being murdered by the same guy she sings about needing her. (I'm going to say he *doesn't* need you, Nance!) Nancy is a character rich in charisma and tragedy, whereas Bet is just sorta there. And let's not forget, I was playing the scene-stealing Artful Dodger, one of the greatest Dickens creations of all time, so . . . Elizabeth's boyfriend? The possibly gay Brad? Well, I think we all know whose stage-door johnny he'd turn out to be by curtain call. Not that I had given it much thought or anything.

After roughly four torturous hours, the show finally creaked to a brutal end, stirring the audience awake enough to applaud before the houselights came up and they descended upon the stage.

This was one of many things about my hometown theater that used to drive me crazy; as soon as the houselights came up after a show, the entire audience would take over the stage like some sort of bleary-eyed, community-theater-audience January 6 insurrection. It would make me fume every night. These people, these CIVILIANS, had zero business treading my boards!

"You did such a good job!" a beaming mom would say to her kid, to which I'd growl through gritted teeth in a volume only I could hear, "It's called a fourth wall for a reason, you stupid fucking bitch."

However, when it was my own family storming past the proscenium to shower me with praise, I had, of course, no problem with it. Or with anyone who had praise for me, for that matter. Or with anyone I was excited to see. Anyone . . . like Elizabeth's boyfriend, Brad.

The minute I saw him nervously greet Elizabeth with plastic-wrapped grocery store roses, my vision zoomed in on him like a sexually frustrated sniper in search of a target. His cheap drugstore aftershave wafted closer and closer as I casually strolled over to stand beside Elizabeth and await my introduction, imagining that the flowers Brad was handing her were actually for me.

"Good job," Brad said, barely looking at me. This led my heart to rev up its fluttering as fast as it would have if he'd pulled out his dick and said, "Room for dessert?"

So when a bunch of the cast and their parents went out to IHOP to celebrate and Brad tagged along, what did I do? Why, ignore him as if my entire life depended on it, of course!

That is because I could immediately tell Brad was gay, and

this was not something I was used to dealing with. I couldn't speak to him or even look directly at him from my seat on the opposite end of our pancake-engulfed table. Every so often, between pours of blueberry syrup and gossip about who screwed up during "Oom-Pah-Pah" (which included everyone, by the way—I cannot stress enough just how bad this production was), I'd glance across the table and catch Brad staring at me. His eyes immediately darted away in that not-yet-familiar gay game of pretending it had not happened, but gayer and wiser than my years, I instinctively knew the rules without ever opening the nonexistent instructions. That night, our tournament of affectionate glimpses was off and running like we'd been doing it for years, with me as team captain of the only sport in which I'd ever succeed.

At this time in history, you couldn't just whip out your phone, follow a person on Instagram, like a bunch of their most flattering photos, and then patiently wait for them to respond to a selfie on your story with a heart-eyed smiley face before promptly responding with a photo of yourself naked. The year 2001 required stealth detective work, like somehow figuring out Brad's AOL Instant Messenger name without making it obvious that I desperately wanted Brad's AOL Instant Messenger name.

As you already know by now, spending hours upon hours every night meeting people in gay AOL chat rooms before taking the leap to AIM for something a little more intimate was as second nature to me as having sex dreams about the Lycra-bodysuit-clad nephew of Donny Osmond that I saw star in *Joseph and the Amazing Technicolor Dreamcoat* when I was eight. But with Brad, I was being presented with a groundbreaking possibility. I had met

Brad, I had seen Brad in the flesh, Brad had seen me in the flesh, and we'd even shared those dueling glances! Hell, he'd heard me sing "Consider Yourself" while doing a jig I had choreographed myself for God's sake! If that wasn't something to actually connect and converse about, then I didn't know what was.

The day after opening night, I devised a plan to get Brad's screen name from Elizabeth. I messaged her nonchalantly, yet brimming with ulterior motives.

MISTERCELLOFAN: last night was sooooooo fun!! did ur BF like the show?

My screen name, "MisterCelloFan," was my attempt at referencing the song "Mr. Cellophane" from *Chicago*. However, I didn't think about it too much, and I certainly didn't look up how to spell "cellophane."

GEORGIABULLDOGPRINCESS: He said he did but he still didn't kiss me. Like what is going on????!! :( Did he seem gay to YOU?

I had anticipated this question and had already come up with a plan.

MISTERCELLOFAN: wellllllll, u know you can tell a lot about a person from their screen name. what's his??

(Said the fourteen-year-old self-titled stringed instrument fanatic who couldn't have told you the difference between a violin and a pair of binoculars.)

GEORGIABULLDOGPRINCESS: Ugh. It's just BradJRomeGA :( that doesn't tell us anything!

Before I could make up whatever bullshit reply I planned to fire off next, I had copied, pasted, and added Brad to my list of follows.

I told Elizabeth I had to run as I closed out our chat window and stared at my friend list, anxiously awaiting Brad's screen name to indicate he was online.

After nearly an hour of staring like a slack-jawed imbecile who doesn't know how to turn on an oven's burner yet is still waiting for the water to boil, the AIM window on my wheezing Hewlett-Packard made its preprogrammed, stomach-dropping, door-creaking-open sound, announcing that Brad was in fact now online. I wasted no time, immediately firing off a message from the cannon of my nascent romance.

MISTERCELLOFAN: hey, this is elizabeth's friend jeffery aka The Artful Dodger LOL! just wanted to say thanks for coming to our show!!!!!!!!

Clearly, besides being a desperate ball of hormonal lust, I also saw myself as a dignified ambassador for the human expression of theater as a whole.

BRADJROMEGA: Hey! Good job! I've always wanted to be in a play but I get too nervous!!!

It just so happened that there was an upcoming production of *Grease* gearing up for auditions. A shiver ran down my spine. I knew I had to do whatever it took to get Brad to audition so that we would both be cast and, inevitably, hook up in some darkened backstage corner like God or Michael Bennett had intended.

MISTERCELLOFAN: ya know . . . auditions for Grease are coming up in a few weeks. u should come!

Brad and I began chatting every night. By the time *Grease* auditions rolled around, not only was Brad in the chorus but, on an overnight trip with a church youth group, Brad sat Elizabeth down and tearfully confessed the reason he had yet to kiss her: he was gay. Sometimes, that's really all it takes: one community theater audition and—boom!—"Put a dick in my butt." Shortly after her split with Brad, Elizabeth rebounded with a guy who looked like a thumb with biceps who played Kenickie. It was a win for everyone involved.

In the production of *Grease*, I was cast in the not-so-titular role of Vince Fontaine, who is one of the only characters in the entire show who isn't a teenager. I reckon the director thought, *Well, this kid is too outrageously gay to have made it to the fifties in one piece as a teenager, so let's make him the lascivious adult*. Vince is the radio disc jockey who hosts the prom and straight-up statutory-rapes Marty Maraschino in front of the entire school to nothing but rapturous bemusement. For no apparent reason, I insisted on dyeing my hair again, this time bleach blond—a blond that somehow came out even redder than the red I'd had for the Artful Dodger. But hey, all great stage stars develop a signature look.

Now Brad and I were in rehearsal for a play together, which would have been the perfect opportunity for us to actually get to know each other in real life as opposed to the hours upon hours we chatted online every night. Instead, Brad and I continued to avoid each other's presence like a dog avoids a bath. I was so used to seeing myself as alone that I had no idea how to behave when we were suddenly in the same place, not one gay guy but *two*. Since I was playing one of the only adult parts, I didn't have to worry about watching him grind and thrust his way through "Greased Lightnin'" rehearsals, but it was ultimately impossible to avoid each other in the cast of thirty. Especially when the time came for a cast sleepover at the home of one the wealthier kids in the cast.

I usually avoided peer-group activities like this, always seeing myself as far too mature to debase myself by utilizing a "sleeping bag" (two words that have zero business together) or spending free time with my same-age castmates. But on this particular occasion, I went because, well, Brad.

There was a big rec room above the garage, and it had that distinct "man cave" aesthetic that should have been outlawed years ago yet somehow still haunts the earth to this very day, like male rompers or Seth MacFarlane's singing career. All the boys placed their sleeping bags around the room, roughhousing and farting all the way to bedtime, while my attention never wavered from Brad. He hadn't placed his sleeping bag in a designated spot yet, and I was bound and determined not to choose mine until I could stake ground next to his. He picked a spot. Then I did. Soon enough the tedious evening dwindled down into a shell of itself, all the gluttonous pigs of my peers passing out into pizza-laced slumber. The lights went out, and after what felt like an eternity, the other boys' giggling about boobs turned into nauseating snores. Soon, it was just my beating, horny heart in the dark listening to Brad's breathing beside me.

I could tell from his breaths that he wasn't asleep like everyone else, and he could tell from mine that I wasn't either. I don't recall whose hand touched whose hand first, but it was one of those beautiful ballets of barely touching. Our fingertips moved toward one another so closely that they almost touched but not quite, both sets of hands on the edge of the cliff but afraid to leap, choosing instead to dangle over the joyful edge. I hadn't even bothered to zip up my sleeping bag before lights out and neither had he, both of us knowing full well this unspoken plan we had both felt since we arrived. The game of glances was well past its second inning. We were both feeling that unmistakable pull to do something with our overwhelming feelings, but neither one knew how to do it. With our hands wrapped around each other's hard dicks, we stayed motionless for a long time in the pitch black. Maybe it was a minute, or five minutes, or an hour, or maybe forever. Maybe there's a version of reality where Brad and I are still upstairs in that rec room, lying there on cheap carpeting, holding each other beneath sleeping bags, and tomorrow is play practice, and we are being forever changed, bettered, and authenticated by our first experience of shared intimacy.

Without a word Brad got up and walked to the bathroom, shutting the door behind him. I lay on the floor, petrified to get up and join him but wanting absolutely nothing else. I counted to one hundred before tucking my erection into the elastic waistband of my pajama pants and sneaking through the dark to join him inside. He turned on the bathroom lights, and suddenly we were face-to-face. I was romantic eye to romantic eye with another boy for the first time ever. We weren't avoiding each other's glances on the stage or at an IHOP. We weren't two hands inside two sleeping bags in the dark. We were simply two trembling boys making direct eye contact beneath the fluorescent light of an upstairs half bath preparing to leap off the diving board to the waters of our mutual sexual awakenings and all the magic and misery that would come with them. Without a second thought, as if I'd done it a thousand times, I dropped to my knees and took him in my mouth and pretty soon had completed the greatest night I'd ever had in my life up to that point.

We didn't speak the rest of the night or the following day until we were both back behind the safety of our AIM screen names, MisterCelloFan remaining the protector of my heart. Trying to speak in the real world remained way too much, way too soon, and way too real. We continued our nightly chats, constantly scheming for perfect moments to meet up in other hidden spots and corners for more. As Brad began to do more plays, more opportunities presented themselves. There was a costume closet rendezvous atop stacks of moldy Munchkin costumes from a 1993 production of *The Wizard of Oz*, along with a tech booth make-out session or two, the loose colored stage light gels catching the light and reflecting little dots of color like Valentine candy hearts on the ceiling as we exchanged our unperfected kisses. Our love affair continued for over a year, though it was mostly a whole lot of talk and occasional action.

It was during this time that I had an enormous falling out with the community theater, which I think it's safe to say we all saw coming, right? They had made the outrageous decision the year prior to let me direct a production of *Miracle on 34th Street* when I was all of fourteen years old, putting my immature and crazy ass in charge of the after-work and weekend lives of roughly fifty adults and children. It was a controversial decision that divided the theater's board of directors, but not only did I get to do it, I did a pretty good job too. The only issue was that now I was a direcTOR, darling! Merely playing a supporting or even lead role wasn't enough for this maestro! When I applied to direct a second show and was turned down because of the aforementioned board of directors controversy, I was enraged. So after a few months of stewing in anger, I did the only logical thing a sociopathic fifteen-year-old would do. I started my own local theater company.

I spitefully titled the venture Antidote Theater Company because I saw it as an antidote to the unchallenging dreck that the Rome Little Theatre was shitting out of their taint of a season. The official mission statement, however, read slightly differently.

For my first show, I picked out a cheap two-person play no one had heard of, begged the local college to let me use their black-box theater in the summertime, then went door to door to local businesses asking them to buy an ad in a typo-laden program that I then printed on my home computer. I sold tickets for ten bucks, and people actually came. We didn't have Rome Little Theatre numbers, but it went admirably well, all things considered.

After that first show, it was time to do a second, but this time I decided to pick something with an enormous cast of kids so all their families would be forced to pay cold hard cash to come see it. I adapted *A Midsummer Night's Dream* and made the cast all under sixteen. I cast Brad in the role of Lysander, one of "the lovers," but directing him, as opposed to just being in the same cast as him to occasionally make out in the prop closet, proved to be far trickier than I had planned. It's very hard to direct someone in a play AND completely disassociate from dealing with them at the same time.

I'm sure some directors know how to do that (i.e., any director who has had to deal with Sharon Stone), but I was new to all this.

Watching Brad have fun with the other kids while I was busy pretending to be an authority figure made me feel even more disconnected from him and anyone else my age than I already felt. Our nightly chats started to wane, and when we did chat, I couldn't help but notice his correspondence had grown much shorter and far less intimate. Something, I decided, must be amiss.

MISTERCELLOFAN: rehearsal wuz great today! how funny are the fairies?! LOL!

I instant messaged him after avoiding eye contact all day.

BRADJROMEGA: Ya.

MISTERCELLOFAN: how was the rest of your day???? anything interesting happen at school?

BRADJROMEGA: Not really.

MISTERCELLOFAN: big weekend plans?

A few deafening minutes of nothing, then—

BRADJROMEGA: No. G2G.

I became more and more desperate, determined to force things back to how they had been at the beginning. I even began planning questions ahead of time that I knew would require longer responses.

Easy stuff:

MISTERCELLOFAN: where do you think u'll live in 10 years and what do u think u'll be doing?

MISTERCELLOFAN: what's the last great movie u watched and why was it so great for u?

MISTERCELLOFAN: write me 3000 words about the color of my eyes.

But the more I pushed, the more distant he became and the more I started to unravel.

MISTERCELLOFAN: can I ask u something?

I broke down and, in a shameful moment of weakness, had to ask.

MISTERCELLOFAN: u r being distant. did I do something wrong?

BRADJROMEGA: No. I'm just busy.

We were fifteen. How fucking busy could he be?

I started losing sleep. I'd stay up all night obsessing over whether he was actually pulling away or if I was just imagining it, convincing myself I was crazy, then hating him for convincing me of something I'd long feared was true. It wasn't long before my desperation morphed into derangement.

One Saturday morning before rehearsal, my mom and dad took me to Waffle House for breakfast. We were seated in our usual booth when I happened to glance out the window. There, stopped at a traffic light, was the sexy, bright green truck that Brad's dad had given him for his sixteenth birthday. I felt my heart tighten at just the sight of it, then the tightening became strangulation as I realized he wasn't alone. He was sitting next to another boy around our age. A cute boy. A very cute boy. A boy way cuter than me.

I froze, a single tear of maple syrup dripping down my chin.

Whatever my parents were saying faded away. Something

inside me rumbled, like the inner growl of a volcano—the sort of ominous moan all the townspeople hear coming from the notorious mountain right in the middle of town within the first ten minutes of a disaster movie before it destroys everything and everyone in a spew of bubbling apocalyptic lava.

"You okay?" my mom might have asked as I stared out the window for who knows how long, but honestly who the fuck knows because I was inside a rage-filled daydream that was suddenly bubbling to the surface. I was imagining myself walking up to that truck, grabbing that gorgeous slut in the passenger seat, throwing him to the sidewalk, and kicking out every single one of his perfect teeth before taking over his seat and driving off into the sunset with Brad.

"Uh-huh," I lied.

My parents drove me to rehearsal, and being dropped off to direct Shakespeare by my own parents because I wasn't old enough to drive myself did nothing to make me feel more confident in the manic uproar I was currently holding to my chest as tightly as a card shark poker player. Blinded by malice, I started that weekend rehearsal the second I walked into the room.

"We are three weeks into rehearsal. Three. Weeks," I barked to the group of children and teens staring at me with mouths agape in a strange sort of fear and pity. "We are done blocking. We are a week from tech. *Some* of you know your lines. Let's just get through this whole thing today without stopping. Deal?!"

Everyone agreed and took their places, visibly rattled by the teen tyrant masquerading as a leader before them. We were rehearsing in the library of the elementary school I had attended up until a year prior (the librarian's daughter was playing Hermia).

We started with scene 1, when Egeus shows up to explain to the Duke of Athens that he's arranged for his daughter (Hermia) to marry one guy (Demetrius), but—uh-oh!—she's in love with another guy (Lysander aka Brad). If you know the play, you know that Hermia is then basically threatened with death or having to become a nun, which you also know (if you're the target audience for this book) is basically the plot of *Sister Act*. Meanwhile, Lysander really wants to marry Hermia and explains to the duke that Demetrius is fickle and the duke is like, "Okay yeah, everybody knows that Demetrius is all over the place crazy." (Who does that sound like?) So basically Hermia is given two seconds to "pick who to marry but choose wisely, bitch."

*LYSANDER (aka BRAD) speaks . . .*

How now, my love? Why is your cheek so pale?
How chance the roses there do fade so fast?

Brad hadn't looked me in the eye since I had arrived, but his energy with everyone else was carefree, easy, even buoyant: the type of energy you expect from a person who drove around in a bright green truck with some other cute (albeit slutty, awful, probably a criminal) guy that morning. *BUT WHY?* My mind raced.

Was it because I was the director? Did that separate me from his joyful mood? Was it because that boy's body was more firm and cut while mine was more wired metal and cushion? My mind was spinning like whatever CD had been blasting in Brad's green truck during his drive-by gut punch that morning.

*HERMIA continues the scene:*

Belike for want of rain, which I could well
Beteem them from the tempest of my eyes.

*I know a thing or two about eye tempests right now, Hermia*, I thought to myself as I pictured Brad kissing that other boy.

Lysander sweetly takes Hermia's face in his hands, looking lovingly into her eyes the way Brad had done that first time in the bathroom.

*LYSANDER:*

Ay me!—

Just then Brad and Hermia began to giggle, that type of giggling that happens when you're not supposed to be giggling. They tried to stop, but they couldn't. They burst out into real belly laughs, which set off the rest of the young cast. A blanket of guffaws filled the room, everyone having a raucous time, and me learning the meaning of "wit's end."

"Stop! Everyone stop!" I shouted from my director's table. "We said we were going to get through this without stopping, right? Well, laughing in the middle of the fucking scene is exactly what we should NOT be doing right now. Understood?"

Everyone quieted down in that way kids do after being reprimanded by a teacher, or by an egocentric child lunatic.

*LYSANDER (aka Brad):*

Ay me! For aught that I could ever read,
Could ever hear by tale or history—

They started laughing again, and pretty soon everyone had joined in. This time even louder. Soon enough I was positively seething.

"TO REITERATE!" I was now screeching over children's laughter. "WE ARE GETTING THROUGH THE ENTIRE SHOW WITHOUT STOPPING, SO EVERYONE STOP! LAUGHING! RIGHT! NOW!"

"Okay, sorry, sorry," Brad said, gathering himself together. "It's my fault."

"Yes, Brad. I know," I hissed.

Everything was briefly calm before it happened again. Nothing specific had set them all off, but they all collectively burst into the laughter they'd been trying to stifle for the past five minutes. It washed over the whole room like a spewing fire hydrant of youthful glee and I lost my ever-loving shit.

"STOP! That's it! Everyone stop right now!" My entire being was convulsing with rage as I leaped out of my seat. "Brad, I need to speak with you outside! NOW! Everyone else take five!"

I stormed into the hallway, cartoon smoke practically emitting from my ears. I didn't even attempt to calm myself down. I knew exactly what I wanted to do. The only thing a rational, professional, grounded gay boy of my age would do in that situation: I wanted to destroy Brad once and for all.

Brad sheepishly followed me into the hall.

"What the fuck was that in there?" I spat.

"We just got tickled. That's all. It's not a big deal." He shrugged.

I looked at him, directly into his beautiful, emerald green eyes for the first time in months. *Wow*, I thought. It must be so nice to be him. So nice to be so carefree and easygoing. So nice to be pretty and confident and cool enough to land a boy as pretty as the one I'd seen in his car that morning. *Of course Brad had strayed to bigger and better boys*, I thought. He deserved it. But me? My earliest fears had been correct: I really was and always would be all alone.

"Do you even want to be here?" I asked, in the same tone as the scorned mom in *A Chorus Line's* "At the Ballet" who just dug another woman's earring out of the back seat of the family station wagon.

"Uh—" he started to answer but didn't finish because I didn't let him.

"You know what? I think it's best for you, me, and the entire production if you just go home. I'll find another Lysander."

I hadn't planned on saying this or firing Brad at all, but the words just came pouring out once I started. For a moment I stopped, questioning what I'd done. I had no clue who the fuck I was going to cast as Lysander, but I was too embarrassed to retreat, so I turned my back and, storming back to rehearsal, *I* promptly took over the role of Lysander myself.

I didn't speak to Brad again for many years. We'd see each other socially and were even in a few more plays together, but I continued to avoid eye contact or small talk and deleted him from my AIM list of friends. And by doing so deleted him from my heart as well.

Despite my volatile emotions, I knew I had reacted insanely, immaturely, and not to mention deeply unprofessionally. I was a child who had no idea just how delicate you need to be when dealing with someone else's feelings or your own. There was no empowering gay teenage love story or road map showing how to exist in the world as a young gay man with a confusing newfound libido, a heart, and a mind more unpredictable than both combined. I was just some colorful kite caught up in the manic tornado that forms when your heart comes of age in secrecy.

I thought that when your heart was broken you were supposed to react like people do in the types of movies I watched every night, like Goldie, Diane, and Bette did in *The First Wives Club*. I thought pain meant retribution. Sure, I wasn't a middle-aged divorcée, but you better believe I felt like one. I had no clue that you could heal in a nonvengeful way because I'd never bothered to watch movies where people did that. Because, well, those movies are boring.

......

Roughly eight years after the Brad debacle, I finally found myself with my first boyfriend. I had just moved to Los Angeles when

I met a sparkling, muscular, olive-skinned beauty named Patrick on one of my first days in that ominous city of palms, poison, and Pauley Perrette.

Before meeting Patrick, I had ended up in LA by chasing both my dreams of stardom and another boy I'd met on Facebook, on whom I had developed yet another deeply unhealthy attachment . . . despite the country between us. Let's call him Marcus. As is often the case, I ignored any signs that didn't point to Marcus being positively in love with me, despite the bulk of our courtship being daily Facebook Messenger chats, sending each other pouty selfies, and a single drunken make-out session at a restaurant in Bryant Park during his visit to NYC that was so debaucherous that we were asked to leave.

I moved to LA trusting that we'd inevitably be boyfriends but I did everything in my power to make it seem like I just happened to want a change of scenery. After one day of hanging out and one night of partying at Fiesta Cantina in West Hollywood, where I was introduced to roughly a dozen of the other boys Marcus was also "dating," my hopes of something long-term were diminished. True to my codependent, bordering-on-stalker self, I clung to this dead-on-arrival romance; perhaps if I squeezed hard enough, I could break whatever wall of reality was preventing him from taking things to the next level. The last night we spent together followed an Ecstasy-fueled Halloween party at the Mondrian Hotel in Hollywood hosted by Adam Lambert that ended with my trying to sleep on a sofa beside Marcus and awaking in the middle of the night to him pushing me onto the floor in his sleep. Even in his dreams, he had "friend-zoned"—or, rather, "floor-zoned"—me.

The next day I ignored all social cues (one of my great skills next to oversharing in book form and making flight attendants regret serving me white wine). Instead of having enough dignity to move on, I instead sat in Marcus's bed as we crashed back to earth from our previous night's Ecstasy high. All the while I practically begged him to love me or fuck me; at that point I would have settled for like me or touch me. In the midst of this game of torture (for both of us), one of his friends bounced in. His name was Patrick. (You met him earlier in this book at the tail end of our days together, so let's now jump to the beginning.)

Patrick was truly the definition of physical perfection. His biceps bulged out of the cut-off Carrie Underwood T-shirt that clung to the slab of grade A brisket that was his torso. The shirt was chopped off to show just a whisper of midriff and a half dozen rippling abs, colloquially known as "six." His redwood tree trunk thighs were squeezed into a pair of cut-off denim shorts, and his handsome Sean William Scott (circa *American Pie*) face was topped off by a smile as bright as the migraine-inducing Los Angeles sun.

"I'm in love!" this gorgeous boy announced in a singsong southern twang not unlike Matthew McConaughey's. "I just fucked the hottest guy in Cali-forn-i-a!"

He didn't seem real. Besides the "sexy good old boy with an air of mischief" shtick he was perfecting, he looked like the type of guy I had watched religiously on porn sites like Sean Cody and Corbin Fisher since the day we got a dial-up connection, mixed with the type of redneck straight jock who would call me a faggot at the country club swimming pool when I was growing up.

In other words, he was hot as fuck and just my type.

"Oh hey," Patrick, a constantly buzzing bee of a man, said when he eventually noticed me.

"You're Jeffery, right? I hear you're also from Georgia." He winked, like actually winked, and on him it somehow wasn't corny. "I'm from Fayetteville!"

The fact that this Adonis was also from Georgia made things that much more exciting—so much so, in fact, that as we began to hang out every single day over the next month, I never once considered actually having sex with him. The idea that someone who looked like him and presented himself as charmingly as he did would be at all interested in me was not something my brain was wired to comprehend. That's probably why I was able to get to know him without turning into an obsessive stalker like Alex Forrest in *Fatal Attraction* boiling a child's bunny in a bid for attention. (That's the closest thing I have to a spirit animal. Alex Forrest, that is, not the dead bunny.) But don't worry, dear reader. I'd find my path to unhinged self-destruction soon enough. But first, romance!

Over the next few weeks, we spent a staggering amount of time meeting up to get stoned in the parking garage at the Grove before seeing a movie. When you go to see a 12:00 p.m. Tuesday showing of *Winnie the Pooh* because you've seen everything else that's playing, maybe it's time to take a good hard look at yourself, but we certainly didn't. Pretty much every morning we'd get up and go on a hike so early it felt like we were going to the airport. We spent roughly a king's fortune on frozen yogurt twice, sometimes three times, a day. We did everything together . . . except make any move whatsoever toward the sexual.

Sure, I wanted him to throw me down on the pavement and ravage every inch of my body while staring lovingly into my eyes and telling me I was way too funny to be so gorgeous, but I never *actually* imagined anything like that would happen. That is until, as in all great love stories, we ended up in a hot tub, in the midst of a terrifying thunderstorm, at the Hollywood Hills house of a random TV executive I'd recently had a "general meeting" with and who had tried to fuck Patrick in the bathroom earlier in the evening during hors d'oeuvres while I was busy with the Camembert. Once we were in the hot tub and the exec had gotten himself so drunk he had to lie down, Patrick finally paddled over to me in the boiling waters to ask, "Are you ever going to kiss me or what?"

With the rain pouring down and lightning striking all around us like James Whale was filming the scene where Frankenstein's monster comes to life, we kissed in the hot tub, carelessly ignoring exactly what one is supposed to NOT do in such weather. The Mary Shelley monster that would soon become our relationship *did* come to life that night as we held each other's hot, wet bodies, the city of my future broken hopes twinkling below this multimillion-dollar mansion preparing to mudslide itself down Doheny at any moment.

We went home together that night and had clumsy sex beneath a poster of a swoop-banged Zac Efron that hung above Patrick's twin bed, then woke up the next morning and declared our love for each other. Where my natural state was to find the negative, Patrick was always a bubbling fountain of positivity. The first six months of our relationship were a daily barrage of happiness.

Both of us unemployed, we filled our days with long drives down the Pacific Coast Highway while smoking so much weed that our glove compartment could technically have been taxed as a dispensary. I thought I'd entered some form of heaven, and maybe, for those fleeting moments, I had.

Slowly, though, we started making video content together . . . which sounds like I mean making porn, but if only. By "video content" I mean bone-chillingly adorable relationship vlogs: both of us wide eyed, Disney Channel–caliber earnest, and clad in the tank tops I'd started wearing in my rapid evolution into Patrick's boyfriend twin. We made videos every day, broadcasting our every milestone or breath, turning our innocent private puppy love into a very public performance of passion.

While it started innocently enough, I couldn't ignore the fact that I saw collaborating together on stupid "comedy" videos as a way of making sure this gorgeous man wouldn't wise up and leave me. And on top of that, I was creatively lost at sea.

I'd moved to LA imagining I'd quickly book a sitcom and cash in before eventually returning to New York City to appear in a revival of *Love! Valour! Compassion!* at Roundabout Theatre Company, for which I would win a Tony. And well, that wasn't happening fast enough for my liking. So, turning my first relationship into my "brand" took center stage. The "content" was influencer cringe before influencers were a thing to cringe at. Our affection for each other quickly became dictated by likes on a selfie, and if we didn't film it, we didn't feel it. The phoniness in our videos was palpable, and the phoniness of our relationship was getting worse with each post. By the end of it all, we were making shirtless movie reviews for a blog called *NewNowNext* and resenting each other's every move. The pure connection we'd shared in those "once upon a time" early days of our falling in love had gone from whatever it had been to something that resembled TikTok long before Tok had joined up with Tik.

Nowadays, boyfriend twin relationships based on viewer and follower count are more than normal (and way more profitable), at least on the pectoral slide show that makes up the bulk of my Instagram Discovery page. But back then? I was a slightly less problematic Christopher Goddamn Columbus of online ego!

Our mutually loving friends tried to inch us toward the inevitable conclusion, which was that neither of us was suited for the relationship we both desperately held on to like it was one of two air-conditioned subway cars when the train pulls into Fourteenth Street on the hottest day of August and someone has shit in the only other one. Both of us, allergic to being wrong and still in some form of love, resisted every nudge and push, and eventually even the glaring signs and exhaustive screams to break the fuck up. Instead of ever acknowledging our problems, I spent all my time curating the images and videos I so desperately wanted strangers online to see to convince both of us we were happy: sublimely documented trips to Hawaii, a video blog at *The Oprah Winfrey Show* finale, photos of ourselves kissing as part of an American Apparel gay pride campaign that put us on a billboard in Tokyo. If you're kissing the boyfriend you scream at every day on a billboard in Japan, and you look pretty doing it, that means you're still happy . . . right?

We both blinked, and what should have been an adorable

eight-month tryst had turned into two years. With jealousies and resentments filling the progressively wider gap between us, it was more than time for something to give. Which, as it usually does, it did. It happened when I discovered Patrick had fulfilled my jealous prophecies and hooked up with someone else while I was out of town.

He was working as a production assistant at CBS's *The Talk*. We shared a car, and this required me to drive him to work every morning as the sun rose over the Santa Monica Mountains. One particularly terrible day, Patrick discovered, upon arriving at work at five in the morning, that he'd left his phone at home. I agreed to retrieve it and bring it to him despite the hour-long commute across town. Back home, with Patrick's phone resting flirtatiously in the cup holder, I began to pull out of the driveway. My paranoid brain couldn't help itself, and I decided to go through his text messages. And this is where I immediately found texts from a guy he had slept with while I had been out of town the previous weekend. In a surprise to no one but myself, I really and truly lost my ever-loving mind.

I parked the car and went back inside the house. There was no way I was making the trek from Culver City back to Studio City after this haunting discovery, especially when I suddenly had a sprawling agenda of tasks before me. The first was to take his phone and hurl it across the yard directly into a stone firepit, where the glass screen shattered into momentarily comforting glitter upon impact. Next, I dug it out of the bush where it had landed and promptly began beating it into glassy sand with a hammer. The third thing I did was call the main office line of *The Talk* where

Patrick himself answered (that was his job, after all), and I unleashed every single rage-filled grievance I'd ever felt in the past two years. It was so unhinged that he hung up on me, to which I simply redialed and continued screaming. We repeated this scream and dance over and over until he disconnected the phone altogether. Yes, dear reader, I once personally shut down the phones at CBS's *The Talk*.

I had snapped. I was once again that monstrous teen firing Brad from the play. The beast of heartbreak that had lurked inside me for as long as I'd had a libido was out and ready to chew not just the scenery but everything else around it as well.

After having to shut down the phones, Patrick realized that the towering inferno previously known as his boyfriend (which was currently destroying his belongings across town) wouldn't cool down until he got there to extinguish the flames one way or another. He took a cab home, across the pre-Uber LA wasteland, and when he tentatively opened the front door and walked inside, I had already taken to the bed where my anger had made its usual transformation into utter despair. After I screamed at him so much that I lost my voice, we both hit a wall of emotional exhaustion, a wall that was so reliably sturdy at this point we could've hung pictures on it. But then again, we were too busy posting pictures online to hang them on a wall . . . because, well, pictures on a wall don't get as much attention.

At some point on that beautiful, horribly sunny summer day, we fell into each other's arms and wept about all the pain we couldn't seem to stop inflicting on each other. Neither of us wanted to hate the other, neither of us wanted to slowly destroy the other, but it seemed we had run out of anything else to do and there was no stopping it. We ended up spending the rest of that sad day playing *Mario Kart* and making up like two children who'd had a simple misunderstanding on the playground. We went to bed early, and the next morning, Patrick drove me to the airport; I was heading to New York to spend a month writing on *Billy on the Street*. We kissed goodbye at check-in, said we'd see each other in a few weeks, and I boarded the plane, both of us knowing full well we wouldn't.

Despite the calm goodbye and the suspicion we were finally past repair, when Patrick *did* eventually call me the Friday after my first week back in New York to officially end things once and for all . . . I didn't take it *great*. A terrible couple of weeks followed where I was a hollow carcass of myself, rarely eating and with a constant stomachache from the Saint-John's-wort tablets I was popping like breath mints after barbecue. I had been in the midst of one of many periods of not being able to afford my antidepressants and had turned to the over-the-counter herbal alternative that doesn't work the same way at all. I was a walking pile of crusty, yellowed laundry, but I got *really* skinny.

Once my gig was over, I returned to LA and an uncertain future. Only one thing was guaranteed: I was ready to come completely unglued. Which I did. Immediately. While Patrick attempted to move on like a healthy person, I documented my every feeling online, and luckily for documentation's sake, there were plenty of feelings to choose from.

The internet had been the place our relationship had lived its happiest days. Having posted our way through two years, now I was faced with the realization that, oh right, we would both still exist but just in separate posts. I'd have to watch as he moved on, and in this case, that happened pretty quickly. Within weeks, he was posting photos of himself, the Pomeranian we'd gotten together, and his brand-new boyfriend who—to make matters terribly worse—had way more followers than I did. They were documenting their brand-new relationship with a familiar ferocity. And with every post, I lost my shit more and more. I imagine it's similar to how Shelley Long felt when she left *Cheers* and nobody was crying, "Where's Shelley?" and instead saying, "Welcome, Kirstie Alley!"

The new boyfriend looked like someone had given a pencil to a super skilled child and said, "Draw a crazily attractive man." He made such effortless sense next to Patrick. Just like how that boy in Brad's truck matched him so well all those years ago. Patrick's new man had the type of sparkling eyes no contacts can capture and the type of muscled, zero-body-fat physique that never fails to make me feel like a wart-covered goblin festering beneath a bridge made of snot. He had that same look of confident simplicity that Patrick had, and he carried himself like someone who has always been hot and never felt weird or left out.

They looked genuinely very happy together as they turned their brand-new relationship into content that rivaled ours. So I made it my mission to destroy them both.

I was extremely active on Twitter and Facebook back then and halted my usually scheduled programming of "hilarious" commentary on pop culture to document my aching broken heart in real time. I don't mean to say I shot off some "oh, woe is me" tweets or posted a clip of Bernadette Peters singing "Time Heals Everything" to my Facebook wall. Well, actually, yes, I did both of those things, but my documentation went much, much further. Too far, in fact.

I wrote a daily blog revoltingly titled *Baby's First Break-Up*, in which I walked any interested stranger through what my ex had done to upset me on that particular day. Our dog, Bodhi, was a big cause of drama. He was a Pomeranian we'd ever so wisely purchased as a puppy on Craigslist, myself strongly aware that puppy content could only strengthen "the brand" but never acknowledging it. In the early days of the breakup, I desperately tried to keep Bodhi as my own, even though I knew on some level I was just trying to win a breakup, not keep a dog. Thankfully for the dog, Patrick won that particular battle and has given Bodhi a beautiful life.

However, the war of the excessively thorny roses was just getting started, and it was anything but cold. I was waking every day in a growing state of fury, firing off veiled threats about posting naked pictures I had of Patrick or slashing the new boyfriend's tires. My *Fatal Attraction* spirit animal had fled its cage and the brand that was our relationship was having an aggressive rebranding. I was generally doing anything I could think of to sabotage my ex and his new fella and, in the process, rub pink Himalayan sea salt crystals into my open wounds.

I was so utterly unhinged that friends delicately tried to step in to help (as I mentioned Gary Beach did earlier in this book). The growing concern didn't just stop with friends: even strangers were doing wellness checks. Like the Emmy Award–winning actress Dana Delany, whom I didn't know but who followed me on Twitter. When the star of ABC's *Body of Proof* reaches out to be like "You okay, hon?" it might be time to step away from the computer. But of course, I didn't.

My acting manager at the time tried to change my Twitter and Facebook passwords, but unfortunately for us both I always figured out a way to change them back and continued to scream into the dark void with my insane tweets. Audition appointments stopped appearing in my email inbox. Apparently, "performative romance" is more palatable to Hollywood than "certifiable insanity."

My mom had standing plans to bring my ten-year-old niece out west on her very first plane ride to visit me during her school's fall break. She and my mom were both so excited, and though I wanted nothing more than for them to cancel so I could continue spending my days and nights harassing Patrick online and slipping into the throes of alcoholism, I didn't want to disappoint them. So I faked a smile and they came to visit.

I learned much later that Patrick had called my mom just before her flight and told her he thought I needed serious help. He wasn't wrong. He explained that he'd begged me to stop with the online harassment, nonstop calls and texts, and general anger being hurled his way. My poor sweet mother took all this in while sitting at the Delta terminal in Atlanta, waiting to fly across the country with her ten-year-old granddaughter to see whatever was left of her beloved and chaotic son.

I put on a brave face that first night when I greeted them at the airport. For the next twenty-four hours, I, a mediocre actor at best, gave an Oscar-worthy performance of someone who has it all together. The following night, after a day at the beach, we cooked dinner and invited a few of my friends over. It had been my first day of feeling . . . not normal, but at least not homicidal. *Maybe*, I thought, *this is just the distraction I need to pull myself out of this sinking hole of despair for which no rope is strong enough.*

Before my friends arrived for dinner, I got in the shower, then the doorbell rang.

"I've got it!" I called out, jumping out of the shower and running over to the door to let in the expected dinner guests while my mom finished cooking in the kitchen. I opened the door, assuming it was my dear friend Jim there to lighten the mood, but instead I found a man I had never seen before. I can't recall a single thing about what he looked like, but I remember him standing in the doorway, now a blank face of pain somewhere in the crawl space of my memories.

"Um, hi," I said, a tad confused and still completely naked other than the damp bath towel wrapped around me.

"Are you Jeffery Self?" he asked.

I told him yes, briefly wondering if he was a fan of the four lines I'd had in an episode of *Desperate Housewives* the year prior. Then he thrust a manila envelope at me.

"You've been served," he declared before disappearing into the dead silence of residential LA, where the distant hum of freeway traffic and the ever-present chorus of chirping cicadas remind you just how alone you really are in the universe.

I froze in place. At some point, probably right away (but it felt like a year and change later), my mom appeared by my frozen side, pulled me inside off the front porch, and shut the door.

"Oh, Jesus Christ," my mom said, ripping the envelope from my hands. "Patrick filed a restraining order, didn't he?"

Before we opened the envelope, I knew that he had.

I burst into humiliated tears and ran into my bedroom so my niece wouldn't see. I wanted, more than anything else in the world, to die. My distressed mother followed behind me, rubbing my weeping back. Through my sobs I heard the doorbell ring again as friends started arriving for dinner while I stayed beneath the ever-familiar weight and comfort of my comforter. Eventually, I managed to join my mom and guests in the dining room, where we all did a great job pretending to have a nice time over my mom's homemade pasta sauce, which I'd looked forward to all week. I don't think I ate a single bite, but I'm sure it was swell.

The next morning, we were scheduled to take my niece to Disneyland. It was a boiling hot early October day in Southern California. It was the type of weather in which you wouldn't want to look at elaborate Mickey Mouse pumpkins on a good day, let alone the day after you've been served a restraining order from your ex-boyfriend. We wandered around Walt Disney's wet dream, me fighting off tears and the type of hangover that could've peeled the paint off the Matterhorn, while we pretended to take in magic and whimsy for my niece.

In retrospect, Patrick had done a lot of things wrong in our relationship, but he hadn't deserved what I'd spent the past few weeks putting him through. Nobody did. And I can't help but see his restraining order as the final wakeup call I didn't know I needed. When we got home from the walking coma that was my day at Disneyland, I stopped the tweets, the Facebook posts, and the cringeworthy blog. I stopped calling Patrick at all hours of the night, begging him to take me back in one breath and threatening to ruin his life in the next. I tried to move forward, one faltering step at a time. I didn't speak to Patrick again for two years.

At the end of that horrible week, my mom and my niece left. Thanks to friends, I deleted all the social media apps from my devices. I got back on my meds. My heart, which had started its coming of age journey in secrecy long ago, had been stuck in that same manic swirling tornado of desperation for a long, long time—long before Patrick, long before I saw Brad drive his bright green truck by the Waffle House window with the cute boy by his side. When you're told that what you want is wrong, it's hard to know how to have it once you're holding it in your hands, and once it's gone, all I knew was to destroy any trace of happy memory that might be left. In the weeks after the restraining order, my life took on that eerie quality that comes after a storm as I slowly spun this moment of toxic sabotage into yet another anecdote in a mind that tries so desperately to turn its relentless toxicity into simple comedic repartee. Scanning the metaphorical debris following my storm, I felt relief mixed with a now-familiar unease that it could all happen again at a moment's notice if I ever allowed my heart out into the wild again. I told myself I never would.

In my room, with an empty space in the closet and dresser where Patrick's things had once been, I was all alone, just as I'd always feared I would be. Yet as I looked around my silent room, protected by a budding drawbridge of empty Chinese food delivery containers and with the lonely chirp of cicadas and the endless faraway hum of traffic underscoring the solitude, I realized that being alone—that thing I'd created so much destruction in response to—was the one thing I'd been needing most of all. As the days turned to weeks, the skies were, for a fleeting moment, perfectly, beautifully, and finally calm and clear. And for the briefest moment, it felt like they always would be.

But of course—because I'm me, life is life, and this book isn't over yet—they wouldn't.

# One Hundred Reasons *to* Sabotage My Life

1. Snakes.
2. War.
3. People who walk around Times Square with giant snakes around their necks.
4. People who support war.
5. The other day when you had sex with a guy who then revealed an aquarium in his closet with an enormous pet snake in it. Fuck that shit.
6. The fact that everyone you love will someday die. Including your dog.
7. Sloppy, open-mouth eaters.
8. Googling yourself, losing control, and reading things about yourself on Reddit—or, worse, the DataLounge—that are even worse than your own suicidal thoughts.
9. Hitting your funny bone.
10. Those shorts that fit last summer but somehow don't anymore.

11. Fruity chewing gum.
12. Not getting the job you really, really worked to get.
13. The time you accidentally fell into a literal *moat* while walking into a sex party on Fire Island and everyone stopped fucking to turn and look at you climb out of the disgusting water.
14. Fighting with someone you love.
15. The fact that you didn't see one of the eight preview performances of Laurie Metcalf and Rupert Everett in *Who's Afraid of Virginia Woolf?* directed by Joe Mantello and produced by Scott Rudin on Broadway before COVID shut it down.
16. Overthinking what someone you barely know thinks of you.
17. When they try to turn perfect movies like *The First Wives Club* into musicals. Sometimes movies are perfect, and we don't need some half-ass bullshit Broadway version that loses all traces of the original magic just so some lazy-ass writer can . . .
18. Wait! Oops. This list is for a different book. I'm sorry. Let's start over. . . .

# Ten Other Reasons Not to Sabotage Your Life

1. Listening to Franz Waxman's *Sunset Boulevard* score while driving in the rain through Los Angeles.
2. Dinner parties at other people's houses (because you don't have to clean up).
3. Pictures of college wrestling.
4. Watching *Bright Lights*, the documentary about Carrie Fisher and Debbie Reynolds, in the middle of the night when you can't sleep.
5. A brand-new set of pens from Le Pen (blue and olive green).
6. When the flight is the perfect length of time to have three mimosas and watch *Tár* for the 434th time.
7. The exact moment in *Hello, Dolly!* when the horses pull the carriage onstage and your heart starts pounding because you know the actress playing Dolly is behind one of the newspapers, then she finally lowers it right on cue to proudly declare, "Dolly Levi!" and

the audience goes completely nuts despite the fact that the actress has done absolutely nothing but lower a prop newspaper and shout her character's name.

8. Eating chicken tenders at Waverly Diner in that one seat in the front that faces Sixth Avenue and has an electric outlet for your laptop.
9. The overture to *Merrily We Roll Along*.
10. Waking up and taking a walk so early on Fire Island that the only people you pass still think it's last night and the deer have yet to be scared off by the racket of men with disposable incomes and Kylie Minogue.

# Taking to Bed

My grandmother—or, as we called her, Grandmommie—absolutely LOVED the hospital. The way some people love to go sailing or skiing, she loved to go to the hospital. There were only two in my hometown, and she could tell you anything you could possibly want to know about either of them. If there had been more hospital options, I suspect her life would have been that much fuller. But alas, we had just the two.

The one closest to her house was Floyd Medical, and across town there was Redmond Medical. Floyd is where every person born in my hometown was born. It is a large, five-story, brick building complete with one of those very 1970s enclosed pedestrian tunnel bridges stretched across the street to a parking garage. For a kid growing up in a town as slow paced as ours was back then, that enclosed pedestrian bridge was like a trip to a theme park whenever you got to visit the hospital. Luckily for me, there were many such visits because, well, Grandmommie.

Both local hospitals had their strengths, but Floyd would have been the clear front-runner if Grandmommie had been a tough-nut judge on an aggressively specific reality show pitting rival local hospitals against each other. I'd watch the shit out of that show, but then again, I'm still watching clips of the WB's ill-fated *The Starlet* series, in which aspiring actresses spent twenty-two weeks auditioning before the less-than-dynamic duo of Faye Dunaway and Vivica A. Fox for a guest role on the fourth season of *One Tree Hill*. The show was a complete disaster but worth every minute for Faye's weekly episodic catchphrase when dismissing a contestant: "Don't call us; we'll call you." For Grandmommie's competing hospitals show, I imagine her sitting in a hospital bed in a crisp paper gown, saying to that week's failed hospital administrator, "I'm sorry, my dear, but this week? You have been discharged."

If Grandmommie wasn't actually staying at the hospital for an ailment, she'd still go . . . for the food. Both hospital cafeterias were among my grandmother's lunch spots in town. She could even tell you which one did which food item better.

"What're you in the mood for?" she'd ask after picking me up from school like a big-city local walking a wide-eyed tourist down New York's Restaurant Row.

"I'd love a PBJ," you might reply.

"Floyd it is!" she'd announce, cranking the car engine.

This was a common routine: drive to the hospital, park, walk in, go past the bloody emergency patients, past the desk where you're supposed to check in to visit a patient, and head straight to the cafeteria, where we'd grab a tray and join the line like longtime health-care workers on yet another shift. Everyone in line had the expression you're supposed to have when at a hospital, by which I mean they looked miserable. Except, of course, for the ecstatic older woman with her grandchild, clutching her tray, debating whether she was going to have the chicken salad sandwich or the BLT this week.

"Y'know they just got a new soft-serve machine? Has way more flavors than the one at Redmond!" she'd brag as if she'd installed it herself before waving at someone in a hairnet restocking a tub of mashed potatoes. "Hey, Suzanne! Good to see you!"

Just as often, though, Grandmommie would be staying at the hospital. She'd end up there at least once or twice a month. Now, this is where you're probably preparing yourself for the terrible ongoing medical condition that this poor woman suffered from. But that was the tricky part of Grandmommie's Platinum Medallion frequent-flyer status at Floyd Medical in the decades before she reached old age—eight times out of ten there was no reason for her to be there. She just wanted to be. It often went like this:

My mom and I would be eating dinner off our bamboo trays in front of whatever episode of *The Rosie O'Donnell Show* I'd taped that day, and the call would come on the cordless landline that was never more than arm's reach from my mother. Or at the very least, her bamboo tray.

"You need to get over to Floyd right away. Your mother's just gotten a room," my grandfather would droll, much to my mom's chagrin.

It was never like the scene in a movie where someone answers the phone to hear the dreaded news that their parent is ill. "What?! When?! NOW?! But she's my mother, dammit!" No. These calls would simply be met by an exhausted sigh from my mother and an inevitable "All right, we'll head over."

On the drive over, I'd beg my already weary mother to let us park in the parking structure behind the Bojangles where the biscuits were better than the Bojangles on the other side of town, so that we could walk across the pedestrian bridge. Feeling like a giant hamster going through a tube was a real thrill . . . if you were eight. My mom, however, was not eight. That would have been literally impossible, or at the very least an incredibly different story than this one (and, let's be honest, better too), but regardless my mother and I are not the same age and for the sake of this book I am sorry about that.

Once inside the hospital, we would make our way through the familiar corridors of sorrow past grieving loved ones and exhausted nurses eyeing the clock till quitting time before we'd reach the big wooden door to Grandmommie's room. Inside, Grandmommie would be propped up in the bed, usually in full makeup and jewelry, with the overwrought dramatic expression of someone starring in a third-grade production of *Wit*.

"Oh Nancy, you came," Grandmommie would muster the energy to say, as if that weren't always part of the drill. It was like gasping in a restaurant when the waiter arrives to your table with a menu, "Oh! Hi! I wasn't expecting you. So what exactly is this booklet? A list of food and drinks?"

We'd take a seat and make small talk as nurses dropped by

with Jell-O containers and the can of Tab with a cup of ice that Grandmommie had requested like she was lounging at a resort in the Turks and Caicos. Then, once it was clear that the overall vibe was bleak, I'd save the day by putting on a show to cheer everyone up. I'd close the door behind me, lower my voice conspiratorially, and say, "I'm just here for the goods." Then, checking over my shoulder like a man on the run, I would steal as many rubber gloves out of the box on the wall as I could fit into my pockets. This would always break Grandmommie's sickly solemnity and get a big enough laugh that I could briefly feel like I'd fixed whatever problem she claimed to be having.

On the rare occasion I wasn't able to join my mom for the hospital visit, Grandmommie would insist on sending home a wad of rubber gloves for me. It was our little inside joke. On one birthday, Grandmommie even wrapped up an entire box of rubber gloves that she'd pocketed on one of her recent visits. I milked the hell out of that reveal when opening the gift as my mother grinned at Grandmommie's hospital jester. Perhaps if she grinned hard enough, it might make it all heartwarming and not just a glaring proof of my indulgence for Grandmommie's dysfunction and a harrowing glance into my future codependent relationships with actresses of a certain age.

"Have they told you anything?" my mom would ask during one of the countless hospital visits where this whole story started off. Grandmommie would look up, with the plain and grounded expression of a hospital regular (she's Norm, and this is her *Cheers*), as she lazily thumbed through a trade paperback romance novel with an embossed title like *Too Hot for Hilton Head*.

"They checked me out, but they said they just don't know. I'm just such a mystery, I guess." Grandmommie would then shrug in bemused disbelief while everyone bit their tongues to the point of laceration.

Usually, after a night or—on a few occasions—two, she'd be released and sent home. And then yet another visit would inevitably be required. Visiting her in the hospital and visiting her after she just got home from the hospital were two very different ceremonies that both demanded bedside presence.

At home, Grandmommie's bedroom was decorated, 365 days a year, for Christmas. It was known simply as the Christmas Room, which was said with the same nonchalance one would use when referencing the den or the bathroom. The Christmas Room was truly that—all Christmas: wallpaper, bedding, rugs, window treatments, pictures on the wall, figurines on the vanity, cross-stitched covers over the light switches. Ho. Ho. Ho. Even the bathroom attached to the bedroom was Christmas-themed, with snowmen and Santa Clauses on not just the towels and bath mat, but the toilet seat cover as well. No one ever commented on it, and it wasn't until I was an adult that I ever considered that maybe it was slightly odd to use cinnamon-scented soap from a Rudolph the Red-Nosed Reindeer dispenser in August.

I suppose the real reason for this year-round attachment to the joys of Christmas was the same reason for Grandmommie's constant "mysterious" hospital visits. She was an unmedicated manic-depressive with narcissistic tendencies who really, really needed her family's attention. Christmas had always brought her family together, so why not keep it going year-round? She'd been born and raised at a time and in a place that never stopped to consider mental health. As she grew older, it only got worse, one unseasonal Christmas decoration and unwarranted hospital visit at a time.

Grandmommie was one of my favorite people in the entire world. She had seven grandchildren (I was the second to youngest), and there was no doubt in anyone's mind that our bond was beyond special. She was chic, colorful, and fabulous: a very short and slightly stout woman with shortly cut prematurely white hair accompanied by red lipstick and chunky jewelry. She'd spent decades working in locally owned department stores—glamorous-sounding places like Esserman's and the Buttercup—that were already things of the past by the time I was a kid in the Kmart- and Walmart-driven nineties. She knew everybody worth knowing in our town because she'd probably helped them pick out the nice clothes that still hung in their closets for special occasions. My grandparents were not rich, but they seemed that way to me because Grandmommie had the air of pure class. I wanted to be just like her. However, I never considered her tumultuous relationship to my other favorite person, my mom, who'd had to grow up under her emotionally unpredictable but beautifully decorated roof.

My mom is the oldest of my grandmother's two kids. Grandmommie was tough on them both, but my mom bore the brunt of it. Grandmommie smelled the whiff of a rebel on my brooding mother, which was the last thing she wanted anywhere near her house and Grandmommie always got her way. She forced her every desire onto her husband and two daughters: whether it was for the type of mood she wanted to be around or the type of day she wanted to have. And if anything didn't go the way she wanted, Grandmommie would "take to bed."

Sundays, specifically, were a big trigger for Grandmommie when my mom was growing up. They'd go to church, have lunch, and inevitably something would set her off (someone not being available to stop by for a visit, a restaurant lacking what she wanted, or simply the prospect of another week ahead), which is when she'd go straight to bed. She'd retreat under the covers with my grandfather doting over her, insisting that his daughters join in the game. When the Sundays got too bad, that's when the hospital visits started. But eventually the hospital visits weren't restricted to Sundays. In fact, a weekday spiral into the hospital usually meant she'd be back home in time for a Sunday spiral into her Christmas-themed bed taking. Everybody hates Sundays, except pedophile priests and people who steal money from church donation baskets, but when you're a manic-depressive, Sundays are the steps leading up to the gangplank of the pirate ship with your arms tied behind your back. You're staring down at the jostling crocodiles of the week ahead, chomping and staring at you with their beady eyes in which you can see endless reasons to lay down in the dark because, sometimes, taking to bed and disappearing into the dark is the only light a person can find. I know this because taking to bed (and a love of Christmas decorations) is what I inherited from my grandmother.

......

My bedroom ceiling is painted gray: a light gray like a cloud that's ominous but not outright threatening, gray like a cloud that suggests a chance of rain but that doesn't scream the certain charcoal black thunderstorm of doom. It's the possibility of rain, the wink that most likely something wicked this way comes. You wouldn't even notice my ceiling is gray unless, of course, you spent days on end staring at it from the bed. Which I do. Often. Some weeks more than others. Those are the really difficult weeks, the charcoal black ones in a life that yearns for crystal clear blue but would even settle for Easter egg green.

My own manic depression has led to chapters in my life where I was completely out of control and others where I've handled the furious whirling dervish of chaos, also known as my mind, surprisingly well. I reckon my most consistent state is somewhere in the middle. My lows are pretty predictable. My triggers include career jealousy, romantic jealousy, bodily insecurity, financial panic, a plethora of shame, and overthinking Glenn Close's lack of an Oscar (fuck you, Academy!). My highs are less predictable and come at such strange moments that I wouldn't notice them if they weren't loud and impossible to ignore, like the guy who has been quiet in the corner of the party all night but who suddenly comes alive after his fifth cocktail and wants to argue belligerently with anyone within earshot about the importance of the four movies Bette Midler made with Touchstone Pictures in the eighties. On second thought, maybe I'm just explaining what I'm like in the midst of a manic high.

Many people fear their highs even more than their lows. But for me, the lows are the hardest. I happen to like screaming about Bette Midler. Just ask my neighbors. I've had mania as long as I can remember, but it wasn't until recently that I began to realize that my way of handling it hasn't changed since I was a kid, and that my way of handling it is to simply repeat my beloved Grand-mommie's behavior. Growing up, I couldn't walk around in red lipstick and chunky jewelry, but I could mimic her in my own way. I could always take to bed when the spiteful shrieking unconscious got too loud.

Like when I lost the role of Annie Oakley's little brother in a local production of *Annie Get Your Gun*, I genuinely asked my mother to murder the mother of the boy who got the part because his mother was more involved in the theater than my own mom was. "You don't suck up enough, and it shows!" I spat at my mother before retreating under my blankets for days, during which time I was nursed back to life like the kid dying of scarlet fever in *The Velveteen Rabbit*.

Or when, after winning the speech competition at my middle school every previous year, I didn't even place, and my mom took me out of school so I could take to bed for a long weekend. In my defense, the topic was "a person who overcame" and I chose Rosie O'Donnell while the girl who won gave a speech about Joni Eareckson Tada, a quadriplegic who became a painter but who was most certainly not in *Seussical: The Musical* on Broadway. I'd love to have seen Joni try to remember all the lyrics to "Oh, the Thinks You Can Think" every night *and* host a syndicated talk show every afternoon!

Or when my father lost his job, and his new job required him to live five hours away five nights a week. When I found this out a few days before my tenth birthday, I became so distraught that I took to bed and wouldn't even come out for the birthday party my mom threw for me in our living room. My cousins and the kids from school played basketball in our driveway all evening, while one at a time each one was forced to present a new Beanie Baby to me at my bedside like ancient page boys bearing offerings to the tomb of an unbearable gay mummy.

In a lot of ways, it's a testament to just how loving and willing to do anything for me my mother really is . . . and sure, maybe while we're testifying we could stop and smell the budding roses of my own narcissistic and self-pitying future self, but hey, chill out. Are we at some sort of smelling competition? The point is that despite dealing with both her tricky mother and my toxic self, my mom has remained pure love. She once even went so far as to tell me that if I ever murdered someone, she'd help me get away with it, which is (a) bad to acknowledge in a book because, well fuck, there goes my alibi, and (b) a simply wild U-turn from a mother who refused to murder the mom of the kid who got the role of Annie Oakley's brother over me. But hey, nobody's perfect. Certainly not the book to *Annie Get Your Gun*.

After raising two other kids before me, my tough but ultimately soft-as-a-towel-washed-in-Downy mother woke up one unsettling day and realized she was living with a tiny hissing tyrant (aka my gay ass) who was brutally honest, scarily sensitive, desperately needy, and piercingly cruel on the turn of a dime. She had, of course, lived all this before. She had birthed and raised a depressive elf who matched not only Grandmommie's Christmas Room festivity and love but her mental unpredictability as well.

My grandparents were diagnosed with cancer in side-by-side offices on the same day. My grandfather went quick: four months with pancreatic cancer speeding at him like a silver bullet. By July of that year, we were shoveling dirt and wondering what the hell would happen next with a very much alive and very sad Grandmommie. She survived her breast cancer but now was lost at sea with no interest in boating.

It wasn't long before her grief turned into a despondent fortress locked to anyone who wasn't her immediate family or a ceramic Santa figurine, with my mom and my aunt serving as caretakers to her institution of need. I was now a selfish teenager and too old to do something crazy like stay over as I had done one billion times before. Soon enough I moved away, off to bigger things and crazier women. I'd always go visit Grandmommie, but it was never the same, not like the old days.

Everyone around her tried to get her to socialize with church groups or seniors or anyone whatsoever, but it was too late. After years and years of depression and a reliance on her partner, her heart was finally broken, and there were no king's horses to put it back together again. Her memory started to go as she became less and less mobile. Eventually she had to sell the house she had lived in since she was an eighteen-year-old bride so she could move into an assisted-living home . . . five doors down. Every visit to her new home revealed that her mind was getting weaker, her makeup less colorful, the room drabber, and her Christmas spirit was dissipating. My mom and aunt visited daily and did everything they could, and still she went downhill fast but then somehow would always get stuck somewhere on a lower ravine, glancing down, daring herself to roll, but bouncing back up, each time a little bit closer to the end. And this lasted eight years.

I happened to be home visiting when Grandmommie took her final trip to the hospital. Over the years, the hospital visits had gone from novel to necessary, taking all the fun out of them. My mom and I were sitting at a local Mellow Mushroom eating garlic knots when we got the call that Grandmommie had had a stroke. This time it wasn't like the days of yore when the hospital call meant attention. This time it meant something worse: it meant reality. That afternoon, I joined my aunt and my mom at the hospital—Redmond Medical this time, not Floyd—and there she was, propped up in bed. It was like the old days, except now she was unconscious and hooked up to all the scary machines that keep the dying from being the dead. The doctors explained that it was time to bring in hospice and to alert the rest of the family she would not be waking up. After all those years of waiting for the other shoe to drop, the boot to her final act dropped with the type of horrible thud that is the fleeting curtain call of life's long musical comedy. A person from the hospice service arrived with a mountain of paperwork for my mom and aunt to fill out as my sister and I sat in the corner of the room across from the snoring skeletal vessel that had once been our chubby handful of a grandmother. Eventually the paperwork that meant finality was sufficiently filled out, and there was nothing left to do but wait. A silence fills the room when awaiting the death of a person who's old enough for it to make sense. You grieve, but you don't wonder, you don't scratch your head at all the years they're being cheated out of. You just wait. I squeezed her motionless, bony hand, thanking her for a wonderful childhood, for creating a secret club for just us two that I could lean on during the countless days of feeling like the outcast that I was. Eventually I took a rubber glove out of the box on the wall and waved it at my crying sister as if Grandmommie might see it and suddenly sit up, alive and well enough again to give me a hearty laugh one last time. Of course, though, she didn't.

She died in the middle of the night, and three days later, I was accompanying my mom and aunt and cousins to view her embalmed and heavily made-up body before they closed the casket and lowered her into the red clay of Georgia. Like all embalmed bodies, she looked like she'd stepped right out of a low-rent Madame Tussauds Museum of Grandmas, hands clasped, wearing as she always requested she would be, a pair of fresh new pajamas and a cozy robe. She had finally taken to bed forever.

As I stood next to the wooden box in the eerie glamour of the funeral parlor, I wondered what she might be thinking or at least what she had been thinking in her final hours or sometime in the past endless eight years of staring at the ceiling of her assisted-living home. Did she ever regret the decades she had spent taking to bed in her Christmas Room? Now with no other choice—an eternity of taking to bed in a wooden box—did some part of her spirit look back and wish she'd forced herself out into the sunshine on her charcoal black days?

Of course, there is no longer an answer because there's no longer a her . . . but as I move on, dusted in her graveside dirt and memories, I keep asking the same question for myself while continuing to repeat her depressive retreats beneath my own plush duvets of manic lows. When I finally find myself in a similar position, yet another elderly manic-depressive, will I wish I'd gotten away from the covers more often?

For a moment, I vow that I'll find healthier ways to deal with my future bouts of darkness. That I'll stop identifying with my grandmother's sad days and start focusing on the bright and colorfully happy ones instead because who knows what endless hospital stays through corridors of sorrow tomorrow might bring. On that next day of emotional lows that seem too deep to handle, I will force myself out of bed, out of my room into the light, and forge ahead with hope and determination.

But then I look around, and I can't find the door.

# Ugh, Gay Guys

Okay, so you know the underwear party on Fire Island? The one on Friday nights in Cherry Grove? No, you're thinking of the jockstrap party in the Pines, which, yes, does happen at the same time as the underwear party, and yes, some people wear underwear to the jockstrap party and some people even wear jockstraps to the underwear party, but I'm talking about the underwear party, not the jockstrap party. You still following? Good. So, when you walk into the underwear party, you are greeted by a team of attractive young men who are paid to live on Fire Island all summer and work at these events. First, you swallow the indignity of handing over a twenty-dollar entrance fee to these young men who, it should not surprise you to learn, are in their underwear and look very hot but also like they've been paid to live on Fire Island all summer and work at these events. Next, these guys stamp your wrist and hand you a plastic grocery bag as they stand there watching you strip down to your underwear and shove all of your belongings into said plastic bag. It's typically very crowded in this entrance area—imagine the unfriendly rush of an airport security line but with the added tension of judgmental gay male strangers staring at you as you basically get naked while chilly ocean air shrivels your balls up inside of you just when you need them to impress a crowd.

Next it's time to enter the underwear party itself. Welcome. You are now an almost forty-year-old gay man in your least faded pair of Calvin Klein boxer brief trunks on a dance floor surrounded by other men of various ages also in their underwear (and, lest we forget, some interloping jockstraps). What's that? Yes, the music is always this loud and terrible, and no, I don't understand why either. You look around the room at hot body after hot body and perfect face after perfect face with the familiar orchestra of your own self-loathing beginning to tune up its brass section. *Take off your glasses*, you tell yourself; *you know you feel sexier without them. Let those eyes sparkle before they become bloodshot!* Yes, it is absurdly dark in here and you are nearsighted with a stigmatism in your right eye, but trust me, you're going to feel way more confident once you take off those fogged-up glasses and let go of your ability to see basically anything whatsoever. See (well, maybe "see" isn't the right word), don't you feel sexier already? Just watch out for that . . . no, that's not Glen Powell—that's a fire extinguisher—but sure, grope it if it makes you feel better. Now that you have the glasses off, you're probably wondering where to put them. Well, silly Billy, you should have left them with your clothes in the plastic grocery bag that a literal porn star handed you at the entrance, but it's too late now, so just put them under your balls inside your underwear. Yes, they will occasionally rip pubes off your balls, but hey, you're the one who didn't trim them, so that's on you.

Standing in a room full of hundreds of strangers in your underwear is quite literally one of the most common nightmares people have, but what makes this nightmare a little more bearable is that everyone else is in their underwear too. Some people are miserable, and some people are having the time of their lives. If you're like me, you'll find solace in the prior and try to have sex with the latter.

Next you psych yourself up to "do a lap." The dance floor is crowded with the worst kind of people, by which I mean the ones who actually like this music, but take a deep breath and pretend to be someone you're not. To your left is a gaggle of perfect muscles, some smooth as a newborn and some with perfectly groomed maps of body hair in all the right places. To your left? More of the same. You will attempt to make eye contact with a smattering of these Adonises (and even a few of the almost Adonises) but their eyes dart away from your stare faster than you can say GHB. Just as you begin to spiral into that ever-familiar wormhole of "nobody here wants me," a man *you* have zero interest in gropes your ass, and you give him the type of cruel, cold glance you've just hurtfully received from the aforementioned Adonises. The circle of life!

You obviously need a drink, but getting across the room to the crowded bar will prove to be your very own Oregon Trail. It will take longer than expected, you will want to give up, and there is a very good chance you'll catch dysentery, depending on what you're into. Once you make it the fifteen feet across the impossibly crowded room, the tedium will continue as you proceed to wait in a cramped line for a solid half hour until finally you are prompted to scream, as if trying to be heard over a passing freight train, "VODKA SODA!" when what you'd really rather be screaming is "A BOTTLE OF MONTEPULCIANO AND A DUVET, PLEASE!" What feels like two hours later but is actually only thirty seconds, a man with a body that makes you want to either kill yourself or try steroids hands you the worst vodka soda you've ever tasted, and you hand him twenty-five dollars with a straight face. You gulp it down as you continue your lap.

The outside smoking section will offer a few like-minded cynics with the added bonus of nicotine and, let's be honest, drugs. Don't forget you're still in your underwear and there's a chilly ocean breeze, so you can't stay out here all night. You're sure to know a handful of folks in this crowd huddled outside the bathrooms, and they're sure to be uncomfortably hiding just like you, so it's a totally valid place to hang out for a while, but be careful you don't overdo it or you'll become the night's "bathroom guy." You know that old saying, "Boys don't make passes at boys who . . . hang round outside of the public restroom doing coke in their underwear."

The only other logical place to end up is the "dark room." Yes, we both agree that this is a silly thing to term a specific area of a club that is already, by all definitions, quite dark. No, there are no walls in the dark room to separate it from the rest of the club, just a row of black garbage bags hanging from the ceiling like show curtains for a terribly lit garbage dump production of *The Music*

*Man*. The dark room is where you go to have sex with quite literally whomever you bump into. I've ended up there with friends, strangers, Instagram crushes, Broadway stars, and even some enemies. The smell? Exactly as awful as you're imagining right now, but multiplied by eight.

To your right, you will see a massage table where you can pay something like fifty dollars to get what appears to be at best a mediocre massage while surrounded by a crowd of onlookers drinking White Claws (aka absolute hell on earth).

You will repeat this lap roughly fifty to sixty more times until it's late enough that you feel the twenty dollars you spent to stand in a room in your underwear was worth it. If you're like me, you will spend a bare minimum of two hundred dollars on drinks by the time you leave. And when you finally do make your great escape, triggered into raw intimidation by all the gorgeous bodies and free-spirited sex you just watched people confidently enjoy, you will walk alone down the pitch-black beach back to where you're staying, thinking to yourself, *Ugh, gay guys*.

You really only need ten minutes max in a situation like this to understand just how often I feel "ugh" around other gay guys. Of course, I'm not talking about gay people in general. I'm talking about myself and the people like myself. The basic cis gay guy we all know and . . . well, we can at least all agree we know one. You know how you sometimes see a cat look at another cat who's being particularly catlike, and the first cat gives the other cat an expression to say, "Oh really? You're gonna hiss at a dog? Cool! VERY original." It's sorta like that. For as creative as gay men can often be, we're extremely good at being extremely on the nose.

What's that? Am I generalizing a vast, varied, and diverse community that's worked hard to get to where they finally are and is constantly fighting to not have everything taken away from them? Sure, but I guess what I'm saying is that for an easily irritated person like myself who's been dealing with my fellow gay guys for over two decades now, we're a lot, fellas. Even after all that time, I still find it impossible to be in large gay gatherings of any sort without getting all sorts of triggered.

My first interactions with other actual gay guys probably didn't help me at the beginning of my journey with gay socializing. That journey, as I've mentioned earlier, started online during that fleeting era of the late nineties into the early 2000s, when AOL chat rooms roamed the World Wide Web.

The concept of a gay chat room first became known to me where so many gay beginnings occur: at a sleepover I didn't want to be at. I was in seventh grade, and I was at a classmate's house. His parents had made the specifically late-nineties decision to put the family computer in their thirteen-year-old son's room. The parents had gone to bed, the Nintendo 64 in the living room was still hot to the touch after hours of *007*, and we boys were tweaked out on Dr Pepper and Domino's and crowded around a humming desktop. In these early internet days, porn wasn't as easy to access as it is today. Sure, you could find pictures of Pamela Anderson's boobs or a photoshopped image of Ginger Spice's vagina being penetrated by Rocko from *Rocko's Modern Life*, but actual straight-up streaming porn like we know it today was a dial-up pipe dream to kids in 1999. So instead, the next best thing was trying to out-shock each other with the type of chat rooms we could suggest going into.

"Singles over sixty!" snickered one of the boys before entering that specific chat room and starting up a conversation with a person who claimed to be a lonely seventy-year-old high school principal attempting to reenter the dating scene after his wife's passing the previous year. We led the guy on for twenty minutes or so before getting bored, moving on, and presumably ruining his night.

"Oooo! Horny moms!" another kid shout-whispered, grabbing control of the computer's mouse and proceeding to chat with an extremely horny mom. At least these chat rooms had accurate advertising.

It went on and on like this, endlessly hilarious to us all. Until the birthday boy, whom I pretended not to loathe just so I could fit in, said, "Click the one for gay guys! Jeffery, you can take this one!"

I'd known I was gay for a while, though I had done the oh-so-common thing of constantly praying to make it not be so. I went to Catholic school, and the seventh-grade religion class curriculum was basically a tour de force of gay panic. I'd hide my eyes week after week in class anytime the dreaded topic came up in the textbook, which was bizarrely often. In a surprise to no one, the people who write textbooks for Catholic schools are absolutely obsessed with butt sex. And hey, I get it! For Lent one year, I gave up fantasizing about men while I masturbated. When it came time to go around the gym and share, aloud, our Lenten sacrifices, I panicked and announced I was giving up watching the VHS recording of

*Into the Woods* with Bernadette Peters until after Easter, which is potentially the only thing gayer than not picturing dudes when I jerked off, but watching that tape was the only thing I was doing more than that, so it was "Sorry Joanna Gleason, and see you after Christ ascends."

The boys at the sleepover were either onto me or just childishly picking on me, or more likely a bit of both. Either way, the suggestion of my handling the gay chat room caused them all to cackle like Bernadette Peters as the witch in *Into the Woods*. (In a surprise to no one, I did not make it to Easter, by the way.)

They must have laughed a little too hard because the bedroom door swung open to reveal the birthday boy's very annoyed mom, who ordered all of us to sleep. The computer was quickly turned off, and I was saved from having to enter my first gay chat room while surrounded by my peers.

I left the sleepover the next day feeling like I always felt when leaving a sleepover, determined to never do something as awful as hang out with people my own age again. But of course, I couldn't stop thinking about the chat room for gay men. Suddenly the bulky Gateway computer shoved in the little room off our dining room wasn't just some crude hunk of machinery on which to half-ass my homework, write terrible plays, and read *Rosie O'Donnell Show* fan sites: it was a potential portal to a world of other people like me.

First I had to get the computer moved into the privacy of my bedroom, which was surprisingly easy. Neither of my parents were interested in the computer, plus the modem was so loud and unwieldy that it only took a few evenings of my clattering away at the keyboard in the other room while my parents attempted to enjoy dinner for me to convince them that my bedroom at the back of the house would make a lot more sense for everyone. Especially me. And the hundreds of gay strangers I would spend the following years anonymously chatting with online.

Once I dove into gay chat room culture, I was hooked. I could spend all day suffering through the debasing task of going to middle school and then come home, crank up AOL, and be anybody I wanted to be. Whatever a man was interested in discussing or exploring, I went with. These chat rooms would lead to the more intimate and romantic one-on-one AOL Instant Messenger conversations. AIM was the single greatest invention of all time before DM-ing arrived fresh on the scene like the sequel to a perfect movie you never thought could be improved upon. (I'm looking at you, *Mamma Mia! Here We Go Again*, and NOT you, *The Second Best Exotic Marigold Hotel*.)

I lucked out pretty early on in my chat room days in a room that was designated for gay teens but was most likely 90 percent occupied by men who hadn't been teenagers since the Korean War. However, that sort of thing never crossed my mind as I was taking everything everyone said at face value. Unlike the childish antics of the boys at the sleepover, I presented my true, authentic self in these chat situations because it was one of the only spaces I felt safe enough to be totally honest. Well, except for the fact that I was an underage boy but claiming to be a very legal eighteen-year-old college freshman. But hey, nobody's perfect.

The way these conversations would work was that first you'd chat amid the sea of other horny typists, usually like twenty or so in total, attempting to catch a person's attention and reel him in.

This was a recipe for chaos as you could never quite tell who was talking to you or who was simply screaming their desire for cock into the online abyss. In that way, it was a good introduction to what it would be like when I started actually socializing with groups of gay men years later. Eventually, in these chat rooms, a connection would be made, then you and the screen name you connected with would branch off into a private one-on-one AIM conversation. This was what happened between JimmyJazz84 and me.

JimmyJazz84 and I didn't waste much time. His AOL profile featured an absurdly hot photo clearly taken on a cell phone, so it *must* have been real. He looked like the type of guy you'd see half-assing his role in a Falcon Studios video playing a college football jock who can't figure out how to replace a light bulb in the locker room who then calls an electrician who promptly fucks him on a bench. He was tanned, blue-eyed, and muscled, with a hemp necklace and bleached blond hair that stood at motionless attention in roughly three pounds of gel in the style that was popular around 9/11. I'm not connecting the two things, but we can all agree that they were both terrible.

He immediately came in hot with the personal information. He lived in Boston, was studying at Harvard, and came from a prominent family he didn't want to talk about. Red flag, you might be thinking? When you're a gay boy in Rome, Georgia, in the early 2000s and someone has abs like the ones in JimmyJazz84's single photo, you don't have time for flags of any color. We began chatting every single night for a bare minimum of four hours.

We talked about how he had grown up in a big family, how he

was closeted, and how because of his excess wealth he could pretty much do anything he wanted with his life but that all he really wanted was to skateboard every day. He was intrigued by me and found me hilarious. It was the first time in my life that I was head over heels for someone, and they were head over heels for me. Of course, it was someone I had only seen one blurry photo of, but what a blurry photo it was!

Soon our online chats weren't enough, and we turned our attention to straight-up old-school phone calls. I'd wait until my parents went to bed, and then he'd call my Nokia from an unlisted number (hot!), and we'd talk and talk and talk all night long. Nowadays, if I were given the choice between having to talk on the phone or taking a nap in the middle of the West Side Highway, I'd have to think long and hard before making a choice. But as was always bound to happen in this great romantic epic rivaling Emily Brontë herself, one day JimmyJazz84 figured me out.

"You aren't actually a college freshman," he told me one night after mentioning getting out of my hometown once I graduated school. "How old are you REALLY?"

This guy and I were sharing so much with each other. I knew how isolated he felt living off campus in the high-rise loft his family owned when all he really wanted was to live in a dorm, skate, and feel like a normal college kid. I knew that he was studying political science, even though what he was really interested in was business because he wanted to start his own skate-wear brand but that his family didn't approve, so he was just going along with their idea of his future until he graduated from Harvard and could strike out on his own. I knew he went to the gym every day, and I knew what he looked like without his shirt from that one blurry photo. So, it was only fair that I be honest too.

"You're right. I'm not a college freshman," my eighth-grade self admitted to this Matt Damon in the swimsuit from *The Talented Mr. Ripley*–looking man. "I'm a high school freshman." Another lie.

He accepted the truth (aka immense lie) and told me that my little fib would never come between the once-in-a-lifetime bond we'd built in the past three weeks but that moving forward he wanted the truth and nothing but the truth between us.

"I haven't been fully honest with you either, Jeffery," he said after my late-night confession, his sexy deep voice trembling just a tad. "I haven't told you who I really am, but now that you're coming clean, it is my moral obligation to do the same."

I braced myself for what he might confess but was ready and willing to accept his truth as lovingly as he'd just accepted mine.

"It is true that I live in Boston and that I go to Harvard," he said. "But I haven't told you my last name, and I've avoided telling you because people always make it a thing and being able to chat with someone as special as you without all my usual baggage has been too precious to give up. But it's not fair, so I can't keep it secret anymore." He took a deep breath before continuing, in utter seriousness, "My last name . . . is Kennedy. Like, *those* Kennedys. Because, well, I *am* one of those Kennedys."

Okay, look, I was a terrible student, but the name Kennedy didn't really muster much for me at first. Sure, I knew it was a famous name of a former president who got his head shot off next to his chic wife, but that was the extent of the American history I had paid attention to in school. So this information didn't really do much for me. I accepted this confession with the same enthusiasm that I would have accepted his confessing to being a leap year baby.

"That's cool," I replied, wondering when he'd send me more pictures of his abs.

He went on to explain that he was the nephew of some important Kennedy. Again, I wasn't really paying attention and didn't really care very much until he explained that because of this complicated family lineage he was rich. Very, very, very rich. Obviously, then, I was interested. Very, very, very interested.

"It's really quite overwhelming sometimes," James ("Oh, please call me Jimmy!") Kennedy explained. "Sure, it's fun to be able to hop on our jet, fly anywhere in the world, walk into any store and buy anything I want, but it also comes with A LOT of responsibility."

I am going to pause here for a second. While I hate to spoil this story halfway through, you have probably guessed by now that the man I met in a random chat room for gay teens when I was fourteen was not actually the heir to the Kennedy fortune. Or maybe you hadn't guessed that yet, and now you're mad at me for ruining the big reveal. But if that's the case, you have much bigger problems than how I choose to structure my little story.

I need to make it clear, though, that I 100 percent believed this man and didn't question what he was saying even the slightest bit. Why? One, he was a good storyteller. Two, I was fourteen. Three, pictures of a good torso can do A LOT of heavy lifting. The moment I should have realized I was chatting with an online creep was the moment I fell even harder.

The conversations went on for weeks, and my life was better for it. I woke up happier. I went to bed more hopeful. I felt less alone. We had phone sex a few times, but mostly it was just the thrill of being able to talk about being gay to another person who felt the same way. We were beginning to discuss meeting in real life. He could fly his jet to my hometown, he said, or could get me business-class plane tickets to see him in Boston. But there was always a different excuse: he wasn't out to his brothers, Harvard exams, the Democratic National Convention. I like to think there were moments that I began to see through this guy's bullshit, but I don't think my brain and heart were wired that way yet; they're barely wired that way now. The ordeal went on and on until I did a well-intentioned (but cringeworthy just the same) thing that I have repeated to mixed results time and time again when my feelings get too big to explain in conversation: I started writing the guy poems.

At first he seemed to enjoy them. God knows I wish I had saved them so I could regale you with them here. I cannot imagine they were very good, more blow-job-obsessed Dr. Seuss than Walt Whitman. As his phone calls got shorter and the online chats got less intimate, it began to dawn painfully on me what was clearly wrong: I wasn't a very good poet.

Eventually, I mustered up the courage to ask James Kennedy point-blank what was going on and if I had done something wrong with my poems. That's when he came clean. Sort of.

"Jeffery, I really really like you. You know that," he told me one night after not calling me for a few days. "But, well, I met someone. He's in town filming a movie, and we've fallen in love. His name is Hayden Christensen. He's an actor."

I was devastated, heart smashed into bits, and I shit you not that the idea that this man was somehow dating the heterosexual star of the recent *Star Wars* movie didn't cross my mind as slightly contrived at all. I fully accepted the letdown and believed him, just as I had the entire time.

I didn't tell a soul, because who would I tell? I hadn't told anyone about our interactions in the entire month of our relationship, and yes, that is a word I would have used with a straight face to describe us at the time. Instead, I did what was probably the worst thing I could have done: I accepted it as fact that someone as hot and successful and famous as Hayden Christensen would always be more desirable than stupid, poem-writing me ever could be.

This was the beginning of my constantly comparing myself to other gay guys, pitting myself against the abs of strangers and letting the outcome prove my lack of worth (let alone abs). It was a dent in the armor of my confidence that I can remember now as clearly as the first time JimmyJazz84 called me adorable. That dent is still there, albeit it's a very stupid dent that isn't as shiny as it once was, but it foretold the way of many, many, many similar dents to come.

My days in gay chat rooms continued, but never again did I let my heart get as involved as I had with my Kennedy. While dicks and torsos still took up an impressive amount of real estate in my mind (let's not forget Brad and his bright green truck), my main obsession became getting the fuck out of Rome, Georgia, and to New York City where I could be gay outside of an online forum. I wanted to leave as soon as humanly possible, which I eventually did at the age of eighteen.

Right before I moved to New York I found a fake ID. Actually, it was a real ID that I'd found on the street outside a bar, and instead of attempting to track down the man who'd lost it, claimed it as my own. The ID belonged to a man named John Glenn, which is also the name of the first American astronaut to orbit the Earth. No relation. My John Glenn had been born a decade before me, making the ID that of a twenty-eight-year-old which I looked nowhere near.

No one was carding in New York in that era, so I had never needed to use it at dinner or the liquor store. It wasn't until I attempted to enter my very first gay bar that someone asked me to show it for the first time. It was at a bar called No Parking that used to be in Washington Heights, a few blocks from the first apartment I lived in. I had passed the place countless times, always itching to enter but always too intimidated to do so. One night, after a few Sierra Nevadas in front of my nightly *Sex and the City* DVD, I found the courage and marched down to No Parking and joined the small line outside the bar. I clearly didn't think any of this through, because when the guy asked me for my ID and I pulled out the piece of plastic identifying me as John Glenn, the bouncer took one look at my baby face and said, "Okay, so what's your birthday?"

I didn't miss a beat, grabbing the ID out of his hands, blushing with humiliation, and just said "Okay, fine" as I shuffled off down the sidewalk without losing my fake ID. And thank God I didn't because once I went home, I memorized every detail of the ID like my life depended on it, which in gay terms it sorta did, and I was off and running.

I didn't dare try No Parking again, for fear that the same bouncer would recognize me, but down in Hell's Kitchen I dove headfirst into the very gay world of Ninth Avenue. My experiences in gay bars before the age of twenty-one are as good a reason for America's legal drinking age as any. No one should jump straight from being closeted in Rome, Georgia, to drinking vodka martinis in New York City gay bars as quickly as I did—and yet there I was. Not unlike my chat room dysfunction, I approached every romantic or vaguely sexual encounter determined to make the unsuspecting suitor fall madly in love with me.

There were so many. Like the Danny Zuko understudy in the revival of *Grease*, which was running on Broadway at the time. He made out with me one night, I blew him in the bathroom of a bar called Therapy (which was anything but), then he lost interest, and I lost my mind with obsession. After days and days of him avoiding my pathetic calls and needy texts, I spotted him at the same bar where we'd met. He was talking to a new, unsuspecting twink who seemed just as dazzled with this generic-brand John Travolta as I had been. So when Understudy Danny Zuko went to the bathroom, I marched over and announced to the dazzled twink, "He's going to fuck you and never call you back," before marching back to the barstool where I was illegally drinking alone. When Understudy Danny Zuko came out of the bathroom, I saw the dazzled twink explaining what the lunatic across from them had just done and watched as they both turned and gave me a pitying expression that will undoubtedly flash before my eyes on my deathbed, accompanied by "Summer Nights."

There was a guy I'd been seeing off and on for a couple of weeks who invited me to sleep over one night. I'd only slept in the same bed with a guy a few times at this point and was more than a little excited and nervous. I ended up sleeping so well that I didn't even wake up to pee. Instead, I *wet the guy's bed*. I woke up from a dream where I was swimming in a lovely warm stream only to discover in complete horror that I was actually midway through pissing all over myself and, subsequently, the guy's entire bed. I sprang up, but once on my feet I realized I had no clue what to do next. The guy was still asleep, but I watched as the giant piss stain grew closer and closer to his sleeping body, like an incoming storm cell on a meteorologist's map. Thinking quickly, I grabbed a large tumbler of water from the bedside table and made a loud "whoops" as I dropped it directly onto the puddle of piss. He awoke, startled, and I launched into a very good performance, pretending I'd merely dropped my entire glass of water in the middle of the bed. Together we changed the sheets and snuggled sweetly on his dry side of the bed. Humiliated, I avoided seeing him again. I reckon a week or so later, upon noticing the now yellowed and imprinted stain outline of my lower body, he must have thought, *Ugh, gay guys*.

There was a very handsome investment banker who came home with me one night. He'd impressed me with boring rhetoric about finance and by the simple fact that his cologne smelled expensive. After we hooked up, we fell asleep snuggling. However, when I woke up, he was gone without even a text or note. I was sure it was just a simple misunderstanding and that he wanted to see me again. He'd even left his expensive-looking wristwatch on my nightstand. *Ah*, I thought, *smooth move, finance bro. Fine, I'm not too proud for a little game of chase*. But when I reached out to him, I got no response, nor did I on my second, third, fourth, or fifth tries. Never one to throw in the towel at the appropriate moment, I started using the watch as a sort of ransom. I sent texts like, "If you ever want to see your wristwatch again, you'll take me to dinner this Tuesday at 7:30." He blocked my number, and I pawned the watch, which didn't even turn out to be worth much money. *Ugh, gay guys*.

Exhausted by what I saw as continuous coldhearted rejection but what other guys saw as simply hooking up like a normal person, I took a brief break from my gay barhopping to settle down into a more consistent dating situation. It was with an equally desperate guy I had met on Adam4Adam. Before we had a chance to learn each other's last names, we exchanged "I love yous" on a bridge in Central Park. I bought us a journal, and we wrote in it every day, giving it back and forth like we were in a Nicholas Sparks story that for some reason includes occasional anal sex. Writing out our plans and dreams for the future together in our shared Moleskine, this guy and I addictively nursed each other's attempts to make a playacted relationship into a lifestyle. Then, on New Year's Eve, we went out for a very grown-up dinner before going back to his place and eating Nutella off each other's dicks. (It's called dessert, folks!) We were nestled in bed watching *The Broken Hearts Club* like we'd been married for decades when midnight hit and it suddenly hit me that I was eighteen and this was all pretend. Cozy pretend, but pretend just the same. I burst into tears, got out of bed, and left without speaking to the guy ever again. To make matters worse, I was also washing Nutella stains out of my underwear for weeks to come. *Ugh*, the guy I walked out on and the lady at my local laundromat both must have thought, *gay guys*.

I dove back into gay barhopping, but I decided to cut out the middle man (in this case, the A train to 181st Street) and just move to the middle of the action. By action, I mean within spitting distance of all the Hell's Kitchen gay bars. My first place was a tiny room with a loft bed so high up that sleeping in it meant making out with the ceiling. My roommates at that apartment were the actor Arian Moayed and his wife, Krissy, who put up with my consistently tardy rent payments until I found a place with a bigger room (and non-lofted bed). That next grimy apartment was above Amy's Bread, with a kitchen window overlooking the back patio of a vaguely nautical-themed gay bar called the Ritz. That was the apartment where Cole and I started making our videos together.

The apartment was oddly big for New York. It was a railroad apartment with three large rooms, a bathroom, and a kitchen. My room was in the front, overlooking the loud Ninth Avenue gay mecca (or hellscape, depending on the day). One of my first nights in the apartment, I was awoken by a shrill drunken voice passing below my window, shouting to their friend, "Oh my God, you've NEVER seen *To Wong Foo, Thanks for Everything! Julie Newmar*?! Fuck you!" I was home.

This home, as it so often is, was a mixed bag of everything I wanted and complete chaos. The lease had been in the name of my newly inherited roommate for many years. She was a bubbly and sweet girl named Maria who seemed to know more gay guys than the Human Rights Campaign mailing list. She lived in the smallest room in the apartment, a windowless space between the front and back rooms that anywhere but New York would have been a midsize closet or plus-size coffin. This room didn't have a bed, just a depressing pile of blankets atop a thin cushion, giving the whole thing the feeling of a dark and damp cavern in a Tolkien story. This room was right off what she always referred to as the living room but was actually just a large room stuffed with boxes, a broken TV, a continent of dust, moldy food containers, a family of mice, and a few throw pillows. I stayed for three years.

Maria partied downstairs every night at the Ritz and was one of the place's most beloved regulars. At first, I loved this direct connection to the hot bartenders and go-go dancers I was too intimidated to speak to. Most nights, a gaggle of these hot guys would follow Maria back to the apartment to do coke until the sun came up and I'd be in the kitchen making coffee. Having to pass by a plate of cocaine right before I tuned in to hear what hijinks Regis and Kelly had gotten up to the previous night wasn't ideal, but I could occasionally convince one of the coked-up go-go dancers to pour himself a bowl of Frosted Flakes and join / hook up with me. There was something about it all that felt almost glamorous to my twenty-year-old self, until it quickly became miles and miles from it.

One night I was awoken in my pitch-black room not to a

drug-fueled go-go dancer wanting to suck my dick but to Maria's voice looming over me screaming, "Jeffery! Wake up! Wake up! There's blood everywhere!" For the record, as far as ways to be woken up go, this one isn't great. I pulled my brand-new duvet as far from the sound of her voice as I could and turned on the bedside lamp. Maria was standing there in her "going out outfit," which was now covered in the blood, which was currently pooling out of her mouth.

"What happened?!" I asked, gagging.

"I was dancing downstairs and everyone was having fun, but then I fell and my teeth broke out!" she told me, opening her mouth to reveal the gnarly row of what had once been teeth but that now looked like miniature ancient gravestones.

"Do you need to go to the emergency room?!" I asked, already scrambling to come up with a reason I wouldn't be able to escort her there when she inevitably asked me for help.

"Naw, I've done way too much coke for that, but will you make sure I'm still breathing when you wake up tomorrow?" she asked with a shrug. I told her I would. And not to brag, but I did briefly stop to make sure she wasn't dead when I tiptoed past her sleeping body the next morning to make my pre–Regis and Kelly coffee. She didn't die, Regis did, but years later and probably missing more teeth than Maria.

By the end of the week, she had a pair of false teeth and was back downstairs dancing at the Ritz, until one night she burst into my room in the same terrifying manner as the first rude awakening.

"Jeffery! Wake up! Wake up!" she cried in the darkness yet again. This time I knew the drill, flipped on my lamp, mentally preparing for more gushing blood, and saw her standing beside my bed. Luckily, there was no blood this time but the same level of panic.

"What's wrong?" I sighed.

"I was downstairs at the Ritz and my new teeth were bugging me, right?" she said with an eerie casualness like it was something a person says all the time. "So I took them out to dance but they fell on the floor, and nobody would help me find them! All the guys are just ignoring me! Come on! Get up! Come downstairs and help me look?"

She was barking up the wrong tree. Not only did I not care one bit to begin with, but I was currently depressed over yet another Broadway boy who'd made out with me, then never texted me back. To make matters worse, he wasn't a chorus boy or an understudy but an actual leading man. I'd already nursed my broken heart with a handful of Tylenol PM, two joints, and who knows how much red wine. I wasn't going anywhere, certainly not downstairs to a gay bar to hunt for missing teeth. I flatly refused.

Her already distraught expression reddened with rage as she stormed back into the hallway, her kitten heels clanking all the way down the creaky old stairs, grumbling under her breath, "Ugh, gay guys."

In a happy ending for Maria, she did eventually find the false teeth on the floor of the Ritz a few days later and she PUT. THEM. BACK. IN. HER. MOUTH!

By the time I was twenty-one and regifting my John Glenn ID to an eighteen-year-old boy fresh out of his own hometown that I was trying to seduce, I had already begun to find gay bars and most overtly gay gatherings to be incredibly tedious. Not that I stopped going to such places. Far from it. Despite my current relay race toward forty, I am still going out and humiliating myself in gay bars all over the world. My passport of mortifying public experiences in gay spaces is filled with stamps, tears, and drink rings from all over.

Like the first time I went to Provincetown and made the super adult decision to do some LSD before going out dancing at the A House, the big bar in town where once upon a time Tennessee Williams met his longtime partner, Frank Merlo. I didn't meet a Frank that night, but I did have a panic attack on the dance floor before retreating to the patio, where I became absolutely convinced that a group of hot guys were talking shit about me. In my extremely muddled state, I decided to pretend that the fanny pack I had draped over my shoulder held a secret camcorder, and I pretended to slyly film the hot guys I assumed hated me. They continued to look over at me with weird expressions and whispers. Maybe they *were* talking shit about me or just wondering what the fuck I thought I was doing with my fanny pack. Eventually I stormed out of the bar, down Commercial Street, and back to my Airbnb. In an acid and gay socializing stupor, I stopped to get a slice of pizza, and when I looked over, I saw none other than Lance Bass in line behind me. Many years before I'd attended a party at Lance Bass's house but was (once again) so intimidated by being in such a big gay group (none of whom were AT ALL interested in my hot takes on Shirley MacLaine's latest memoir) that I hid in the bathroom before sneaking out the back door. Years later in P-town, I was convinced Lance Bass recognized me and somehow remembered my hiding in his bathroom. (And we've literally never said more than a hello to each other.) I threw my money on the counter and took off like some sorta gay social fugitive. The one good thing about that experience in social panic was that there was a huge COVID outbreak on the dance floor that night, and being kept outside by my social anxiety (and heavy LSD tab) actually prevented me from catching the Cape Cod debut of the Omicron strain, so . . . a win?

Not losing my shit in these situations is something I've worked on in therapy for many years, and I've actually made a lot of progress. Sure, sometimes I slip up. Like when I ended up at a very sweaty, sexy dance party in Palm Springs and attempted to smooth-talk an especially sexy man while smoking a cigarette in the parking lot. I thought I was leaning suavely against a wall but was actually just falling into a cactus. The hot guy walked away mortified, and I had to lie down while friends held a camera light over my head and pulled out five enormous spikes that were stuck into my skull. (Three days later, while taking a shower, I found two more still lodged in my head.) I have finally started to learn that I must really and truly mentally prepare for large gay groups because they are nothing if not a carousel of triggers.

It makes sense that these types of scenarios trigger and intimidate me and make me spin out of control. When gay people finally find a community after being raised to constantly feel othered for simply being who we are, of course the first thing we do is search for ways to further other ourselves from our own. There will always be someone hotter, more successful, more in love, funnier, more popular, richer, in better shoes, whatever. Maybe we're not all a straight party girl scuttling around the dance floor of a gay bar searching for her false teeth while the gays ignore her, or a manic gay thirtysomething trying to impress a man with biceps the size of his head before falling into a literal cactus. But I have yet to meet another gay guy who doesn't spin out at least a little bit in these situations.

The desperate feeling of wanting to belong after decades and decades of growing up an outsider leads you to always doubt you belong, even when you do. And when you want something that much, need something that much, a boy leaving in the middle of the night without saying bye, or a person rolling their eyes at you from across a crowded club when you're tripping on LSD, can feel like you've been sucked into a time machine and you're suddenly a kid desperately hoping to find another person like you in your conservative small town, a kid getting his heart broken by a Kennedy in a chat room. Maybe it's from building up these types of situations my whole life, but when in them and the tiniest thing makes me feel like I'm an outcast, I immediately go back to that feeling of *ugh, gay guys*. We all just want to belong, but in my case, at least, I thrive at being my absolute worst enemy.

But then again, there's the opposite. There's that moment after the Fire Island underwear party when you've finally made it back to the house you're staying in with your friends. You're all exhausted from both the triggering and the magical moments that have filled your night. You're all sitting around on the sofa eating chips, out-shocking each other with what you just did, and passing around a joint. The TV is turned on, and the clips begin. Suddenly any negativity from earlier fades away as you and your friends are screaming along to a video of the 1976 Tony Awards performance of *A Chorus Line*, and absolutely everyone knows the words. You remember you're a part of a community that is far bigger and brighter than any trigger could ever be. You tell yourself you must stop looking for ways to be othered and simply embrace it. You did it. You got the fuck out of your hometown, and you made it to a place with other people who grew up loving Bernadette Peters in *Into the Woods* just as much as you. You're safe now, you're inside, and no matter how many cactuses you fall into, no matter how many guys intimidate you . . . you belong.

*Ugh*, you think with a smile and a flutter of joy as you look around the room at your community of friends, *gay guys*.

# George and Martha, Sad Sad Sad

My husband, Augie, and I kicked off our honeymoon in Puerto Vallarta at a hotel that had been built by Richard Burton as a house for Elizabeth Taylor. We spent our first night getting shit-faced in bed while we watched the two of them in *Who's Afraid of Virginia Woolf?* That was the best way we could imagine celebrating marriage.

Somehow, I've spent more than five years married to one of the cutest and most charismatic British men who's ever walked the earth. His name is Augustus Art Prew, which I'd say was the most absurdly British name there's ever been, but his brother's name is Somerset Sidney Prew. Augie and I met eight years ago at a brunch where we hooked up in the bathroom and have basically been together ever since.

But before Augie, I should tell you about Joel, the guy I was dating when I met Augie and—spoiler alert!—whose heart I broke. If there's one thing I'm good at, it's making a huge mess. And hooking up in bathrooms. Often at the same time. Heyo! Tip your waitresses, folks!

I met Joel Creasey in Sydney, Australia, when I was there for a month performing a show with Cole during Sydney's big gay Mardi Gras festival. I spent every night of my first couple of weeks going to gay bars after our show, attempting to hook up with at least one new stranger or else I'd go to bed feeling like a failure. Or worse: unattractive. I was in my midtwenties, fit, better-medicated than the last time I'd been single, and having a hell of a time. Of course, at some point I became infatuated with a very handsome guy named Jack, whom I started obsessively building my days around, hoping he'd text and following him to parties I had zero interest in attending. Sure, we had literally nothing in common, but he was extremely sexy, Australian, ripped, a surfer, and rich. I'd include a photo of him to really drive this point home, but that would require reaching out to him, and I can only imagine he's blocked me on Instagram after one too many late-night drunken lovesick DMs over the years.

It was during my last week in Sydney that things with Jack came to the inevitable end I had so diligently avoided considering. I had been getting progressively clingier. I brought him onto a sailboat with Cole, Cole's boyfriend at the time, and the brilliant actor / drag star Trevor Ashley. It was a stunning day sailing across Sydney Harbor, but I spent it being depressed that Jack wasn't bursting into tears over the fact that I'd be gone by the end of the week. Instead he was—gasp!—just enjoying his day.

After that needy boat trip, I decided to have some self-respect and take a night off from Jack and do something without him, by which I mean he was busy. I went to a house party with a gay comic I knew through Instagram, and when I arrived, my eyes immediately fell upon a beautiful blond boy with heavy eyelids and lips that seemed drawn on with a red Crayola. To make matters even more alarming, he was sarcastic, equally over the absurdity of going out to a club as I was, and a very well-known comedian in Australia. This was Joel Creasey. We departed for the club, and by midnight we were ghosting the consummate drag superstar Jinkx Monsoon mid-drinks, buying lube from a nearby corner store, and heading back to my place.

The following day I said goodbye to Jack, by which I mean I begged him to fuck me and cried when I came all over his mattress. My semen hadn't even finished staining his sheets before I'd moved my obsessive habits to Joel. When he and I tearfully said goodbye in Sydney, we were one martini away from saying "I love you." Two days after I returned to LA, Joel bought me a plane ticket to return to Australia to see him perform at the Melbourne Comedy Festival.

A couple of weeks later, I flew back to Australia and spent two weeks with Joel. He showed me all around Melbourne, where his adorable face was plastered across the city. It advertised his sold-out show, which was to take place above a Swiss restaurant serving food that seemed to go out of its way to be uniquely terrible. I was, as usual, completely broke. I can't remember if I hadn't been paid for my month performing in Sydney or if I'd already blown it on weed and a late-night eBay purchase of a rare *She-Devil* movie poster that I had professionally matted and framed before bothering to pay my car insurance. (I'm leaning toward the latter. How about you?) Joel looked after me and treated me to fancy meals and a chic trip out to Australian wine country, where we found ourselves drunk on a pier overlooking a beautiful sunset. While we'd been one martini away from saying "I love you" that first weekend together, we were now Sauv Blanc-ed enough to say it this time—and say it we did.

The rest of our weekend together was just as Jackie Collins–level romance. We had the enormous cabin to ourselves the first night, and we hooked up on every available surface and in every body of water: shower, hot tub, pool, dishwasher. (Okay, fine, not the dishwasher; I'm just making sure you're paying attention.) Then a gaggle of Joel's friends joined us for the rest of the weekend. We did nothing but go to wine tastings, laugh, and memorize all the lyrics from the *Sister Act, The Musical* cast recording. I felt a billion miles away from anything and anyone I knew. I was that ideal version of myself you can feel only when you're dislocated from your life and pretending to be your best self.

That quickly became one of many draws to my relationship with Joel. He lived on the other side of the world, and when we'd convene, it would always be a vacation. He came to California, and we escaped to Palm Springs, where we got into a furious argument with the front desk at the Ace Hotel because of too many noise complaints. These stemmed from my blaring and screaming at the pilot episode of Debra Messing's *The Mysteries of Laura* the night that it premiered. Somehow we got a free room voucher out of it and returned on Joel's following trip. And that's more than Debra Messing can say she got out of *The Mysteries of Laura*.

We met up in London for New Year's before traveling to Berlin with Joel's family. Our second night, we went out to a notorious gay sex club, where we tried to buy cocaine off a guy we met in the dungeon's sex sling, but when I followed him to the bathroom, he started shooting up heroin as casually as someone using a Q-tip. I'd never seen someone do that in real life before (shoot heroin, that is, not use a Q-tip), and I literally screamed and ran into the streets, never to return to the club. The next night we went to a Christmas market, then had dinner with Joel's family at a fancy restaurant recommended to me by Dana Delany. It was an eclectic itinerary.

We rendezvoused in New York, where he opened for Joan Rivers (her last performance—she died a few days later), and I got so characteristically jealous that I refused to take a sightseeing helicopter ride with his family the following morning. I blamed it on a hangover.

All this is to say that (a) every time we hung out, it was in the midst of a vacation or trip, and (b) who wouldn't want to date me?!

Joel and I had been "open" from the start as our continental divide required such a thing, but the rule was no emotional attachment. I was and remain pretty lazy when it comes to hooking up with other people outside a relationship. I was getting the romantic validation that comes from heartfelt text messages and sappy FaceTimes, all without having to douche. Sure, I'd make out with a guy at Akbar every so often or meet up with a fuck buddy, where the routine was so well rehearsed that it was basically clinical. Well, as clinical as something can be when you're handcuffed and getting fucked by a guy while he ignores you and watches football, a guy whose name you forgot the first time so haven't been able to ask in all the years of having sex that followed. Including just this past summer, when you saw him at Drag Bingo in Cherry Grove and recognized him solely by his back tattoo. Ah, being gay.

After a while, I started getting bored of our long-distance thing and yearned for a connection that didn't involve air travel. Also, as comforting as it was to imagine running away from everything I knew and starting over as the trophy husband of a successful Australian comedian, I knew that was never going to happen. Hot weather at Christmas? Fuck off.

I am not very good at confrontation (unless you're the front desk of the Palm Springs Ace Hotel and Debra Messing is back on NBC), so anytime I tried to broach the subject that this was a ridiculous thing for us to be doing with our lives, I ended up caving. If he cried or even vaguely frowned, I'd go from "This isn't working" to "Would your relatives in Perth find an Olivia Newton-John–themed wedding gauche or patriotic?"

But then I met Augie.

And this brings us to Roland Emmerich's Fourth of July pool party, where I am sure many great gay romances have begun. Roland Emmerich is the director of (among many things) *Independence Day* and that flop about the Stonewall riots where a young white twink was depicted as having thrown the first brick, played by, of course, a straight actor with a famous dad. All in all, a pitch-perfect Hollywood setting for my first almost interaction with the man who would eventually become my husband.

It was the type of very hot and dry Southern California day that creates forest fires and makes you question your decision to have stayed on the West Coast for so many years despite not having become the success you had planned on when you still believed in yourself. I was dog-sitting for the weekend at my friend Jim's, mainly because he had central AC and I did not.

My friend Jordan Firstman and I kicked off the weekend by going to a big party in Venice thrown by someone neither of us knew. We spent the entire evening in the garage cornering and worshipping Thandiwe Newton for what can't have been less than two hours (she didn't seem to mind). When we got back to Jim's later that night, we sent photos of ourselves watching her in *Mission: Impossible 2* and *Norbit* to her number, which she had (unwisely) shared with us. We never heard from her ever again, and now that I'm thinking about it, it probably wasn't even her real number, so who the hell did we send selfies in front of *Norbit* to?! Another question for another day, Jessica Fletcher.

The following day was even hotter, so Jordan and I took to Instagram and Grindr in an attempt to find a pool party. Someone told us that there was a huge party happening at Roland Emmerich's house in the Hollywood Hills and that they doubted two gay twentysomethings would be turned away. You don't discuss or debate this sort of thing; you simply get in the car and drive to the address the person you sorta know on Instagram gave you. When the security guard asked for our names, Jordan gave them. The guard checked and told us, "You're not on the list." Jordan confidently and casually put his hand to his chest in mock surprise and scoffed, "*We* aren't on the list?" and the guy immediately let us in. That's Hollywood, baby.

The party was packed full of gay guys who had undoubtedly gotten past security in a similar fashion. Absolutely no one was in the pool, instead choosing to pose beside it. Liam Hemsworth was there dancing with the girl from *It Follows*. Vivica A. Fox was wandering around the open bar saying, "I'm too blessed to be stressed." Roland Emmerich wasn't even there, and some random staffer was the one hosting the whole thing. Actually, *that's* Hollywood, baby.

Jordan and I stayed at the party for a while, running into our friend Jeremy, who kept trying to flag down his friend Augie. It was too crowded, and we never ended up finding Augie because we eventually ducked out to watch the fireworks on a roof across town with more people we barely knew, which meant we missed out on the inevitable sex fest that occurred in the pool after all the celebs had left.

The following morning, Jordan and I took our extremely hungover selves over to an apartment where Jeremy and his friend Augie were cooking brunch. They asked us to pick up champagne and orange juice for mimosas, but seeing as neither Jordan nor I had more than forty dollars in our checking accounts between us, we spent exactly forty dollars on champagne and skipped the citrus. The moment we stepped into the cramped Silver Lake apartment, we were met with the always-comforting (when you're as hungover as we were) smell of frying bacon and eggs. And that's when Augie poked his head out of the kitchen and said "Morning" in his cute accent and with the unrelentingly Puck-like and sparkly energy I would soon learn a human being can actually possess without narcotics. Though they certainly help. Augie was dressed in what can only be described as a billowy patterned tunic and flowing patterned pants that completely clashed in the most perfectly high-fashion way. His shoulder-length hair was tied up in a messy topknot, his feet were bare and filthy, his skin as effortlessly smooth and tanned as a Grecian olive farmer, and I thought, *Who the hell is this gorgeous pirate, and why is he overcooking my eggs?*

The mission of my day quickly shifted from getting free brunch to making this gorgeous pirate be impressed by me. I made a beeline to sit next to him on the floor as we crowded around the coffee table. There wasn't enough food, and as the champagne kept popping and the spliffs kept passing, we were all getting hungrier. In an effort to impress the topknotted Puck with the sexy British accent, I announced that I would tweet that I was broke and needed pizza and ask for someone to send it, proudly claiming I could make it happen. Now of course, in retrospect, this is deeply cringe. No, I don't just mean being on Twitter at all; I'm referring to this sort of crowdfunded way of living that I regretfully fell into the habit of from time to time. You'll be happy to know that I've never done anything like that again, nor am I even on Twitter after one too many searches for my own name and the humiliatingly low number of results that sent me spiraling. But more important, my waist isn't small enough now for anyone to actually believe I'm hungry and in need.

Regardless, a stranger sent pizza to the apartment within ten minutes, and Augie was impressed enough by my tenacity/desperation to go into the bathroom and hook up with me. It wasn't long before we were back where I was house-sitting, holding each other on the sofa, stoned out of our minds, and watching *Showgirls* in the dark before eventually fucking. All in all a lovely foreshadowing of how our future would look. The next day I left the house in such haste that I forgot to remove the dirty sheets off the bed, and when my friend Jim returned home, he texted me pointing out this very crusty fact, to which I responded, "Oh sorry about that! I had a terribly runny nose all weekend!"

After that first day and night together, I couldn't stop thinking about Augie. I'd been very up-front about the fact that I had a boyfriend who was, yes, far away but also arriving two days later. Oh right, I forgot to mention that part of the story up top. Two days after I met Augie, I was scheduled to pick up Joel from the airport, where he would be flying in to see the premiere of the horror movie I'd made with a bunch of friends called *You're Killing Me*, at Outfest (the gay film festival in LA). The whole thing was one of those red-letter days that you want your long-distance boyfriend to attend . . . but also the guy you hooked up with in the bathroom at brunch.

The day after our first night together, Augie and I went on a "proper date," which was immediately breaking the vague rules of my open relationship with Joel, but like everything in my life, once I push an envelope, it's never long before I end up shoving a full UPS package next. The date was a hike, which is one of the many drawbacks of living in Los Angeles. We went to Altadena and hiked up a mountain (for a much longer duration than Augie had originally claimed, not necessarily a red flag but a millennial pink ribbon at the very least). The hike snaked up a very steep mountain to the grounds of a hotel that had burned down sometime in the history of LA that no one cares about (which is basically two days ago). Once we reached the peak, we laid our exhausted bodies down on the cement steps that had once led to a fabulous ballroom and looked down over East Los Angeles.

On the way up the mountain, we'd been in that full pseudo-hippie style you're almost required to enter when you're on a first date in Los Angeles: discussing pasts, "journeys," and signs from the universe. It's the type of cliché shit that makes a person want to punch the speaker in the face unless they're Goldie Hawn, in which case . . . carry on, my angel of betterment. Can I get you a tea or a green juice?

I went into a long-winded tale about how when I decided to drop out of drama school the only person I spoke to about it was my Stanislavsky teacher, Tanya Belov. Tanya was this deeply intimidating Russian woman who (along with her husband, Yuri) had left her position at the Moscow Clown Theater to come to America. They'd somehow ended up teaching at the University of North Carolina School of the Arts in the early eighties. Tanya was still an acting teacher when I started there as a freshman in the fall of 2004. She and I quickly clicked (I would later learn this was always the case with the obviously gay boy in the class; I wasn't special, just predictably limp-wristed and bitchy). If she wasn't on her feet lecturing, she'd beckon me to sit beside her in class, where we would write notes back and forth to each other in my notebook like naughty fifth-graders.

She knew I wasn't happy there for many reasons, the biggest being that after four years of homeschool I was having a hard time being a small fish in a big pond—or stepping into a pond of any size, for that matter. When you float on lazy afternoons watching daytime TV for four years, it's hard to swim your way through a challenge of any kind. When I finally decided to leave drama school, I asked Tanya to lunch to tell her. We were to meet on the balcony of the food hall, and as I nervously made my way there, I noticed a trail of orange peels, as if someone had slowly peeled the fruit on their stroll across campus. When I found Tanya at the table, she was, of course, eating a perfectly peeled orange, and she knew exactly what I was there to say.

Back on the mountain in Altadena, I had finished telling this story to Augie, adding that ever since that day in North Carolina, I always notice random orange peels on the ground when I'm at the precipice of some big life change. And that's when we had made it up to the old hotel grounds and found, scattered across the remnants of the old stone steps, tons of orange peels.

Augie and I laughed at the synchronicity of it all before we lay on the steps to catch a breath and fill our lungs with marijuana. We hadn't kissed or touched the whole day, but as we lay in the shade atop the coolness of the stone, we rolled over and kissed, surrounded by orange peels, and I knew right then and there . . . I was in big trouble.

Now, we were one day away from Joel's arrival, and when I dropped Augie off at his place, he told me he completely understood the situation and that he was going to give me the space to figure out what I wanted. He told me that if I wanted to hang out again down the road, he would be around, but if not, he would happily just be friends.

The next day I picked up Joel from the airport, but before I did, I made the bizarre decision to change Augie's saved number in my phone from "Augie" to "Granddad." My thinking was that if Joel were to be suspicious (I had tried to break things off at least four times by this point) and went through my phone, he wouldn't think to stop and read whatever I was texting to my grandfather (who had been dead for well over a decade at that point).

Joel and I spent his first day on the beach in Malibu, then had dinner at Lisa Vanderpump's Villa Blanca (RIP), where he (possibly) got food poisoning (which maybe explains the restaurant's RIP). The following evening was the movie premiere, and I'd been in full manic up excitement mode that whole day as we prepared. Perhaps, if I hadn't been in such a manic up, I might have noticed that things were off between us, but I didn't because my manic ups have a way of turning any questionable moment into an exclamation point holiday.

It was a wild, revelatory night in front of a sold-out audience of friends and strangers. Needless to say I was in heaven and chased the screening with a big boozy party at a downtown gay bar. Sometime after Joel and I had gotten back to my place, I passed out in bed and started talking in my sleep, which I have a tendency to do. On this particular occasion, I started talking about Augie, and unfortunately for everyone involved, Joel was very much not asleep.

I awoke the next morning with Joel's pensive face staring at me.

"Who's Augie?" he asked flatly.

*Oh shit*, I thought in panic.

"Hmm?" I replied in fictitious calmness.

"Is he the person you named Granddad in your phone?" he asked in that stilted way people do that tells you you're really fucking fucked. "You've been so weird since I got here, and last night you started talking in your sleep about someone named Augie and how much you wished he had been there last night. So then I went through your phone and didn't see anyone named Augie but then I saw you'd texted your granddad that you wished he'd been at the movie and I thought, *His granddad is fucking dead, and that was a super gay movie*. And then I kept reading . . ."

I cut him off. I couldn't let him explain that he'd read an earlier text I'd written to my "granddad" about how intense my feelings were for him every time we kissed but how I needed to figure things out so no one got hurt. *Who?* Joel must have briefly wondered. *Your grandmother?!*

I explained all the obvious reasons—we were open, he lived on the other side of the world, we were too young for this type of thing, we rarely saw each other—all of which were squashed by his asking, or rather screaming, "Yes, but WHY DID YOU LET ME FUCKING FLY HERE?!"

I didn't have an answer for that one other than the fact that I was a selfish jerk who couldn't handle confrontation of any kind and that I had an uncanny ability to incinerate everything I touch, burning not just myself but everyone around me in the process. Midas meets Drew Barrymore in *Firestarter*.

Luckily, I didn't have to say any of that icky self-reflective jargon because Joel was already packed up and rushing out the door to a waiting Uber, before screaming at me one last time across the front yard for all my neighbors to hear: "YOU'VE BROKEN MY

FUCKING HEART!" And it sounded even more dramatic with his precious Australian accent.

The rest of that day was a write-off. I had never broken up with someone before, I felt like shit, and each enraged text message Joel sent made me feel rightfully worse. I entered a weird trance of both guilt and relief, so I did what anyone would do and got under the covers and listened to the audio book of *Eat, Pray, Love* for the fortieth time before rewatching the movie for the . . . actually, I can't comfortably confess in print the number of my previous viewings.

Joel was now hunkering down at a hotel in Santa Monica. He was already scheduled to fly to New York at the end of the week, so after a couple of days, the initial chaos and anger receded enough that he came back to spend his last night at my place before I took him to the airport the following morning. It was as awkward an evening as I've ever encountered (and I saw Wendy Williams in *Chicago*), but we managed to sit on the sofa together all night, guzzling wine and eating tacos while watching YouTube clips of the BBC reality show *I'd Do Anything*, in which a dozen belting broads battled it out on national television for the chance to play Nancy in a revival of *Oliver!*, complete with Andrew Lloyd Webber in the Simon Cowell judge's chair. I was falling more and more in love with the Brits by the second.

Joel slept in my bed, and I slept on the sofa that night. We got up early so I could drive him to LAX. Both of us were in tears as we said our goodbyes while barreling down the 405, but on some level, I could tell that Joel understood. He is a deeply intelligent person whose fantastic career in Australia was just beginning to blow up. He was never going to walk away from that, and I was never going to walk away from the charred hellscape that was my own career at that time. What we'd had was truly special, but it wasn't reality. It wasn't pretend either, but something in the middle, that yummy feeling in your toes when you're on vacation somewhere far from home and you think, *This version of myself wears suspenders all week*. Then you get home and you try to wear the vacation suspenders again, and sure, it was cute to try something new when you were in Sacramento, but now you look at yourself and realize you're not actually the guy who wears suspenders. (For the record, I would sooner jump into a bucket of broken glass than wear suspenders, and I've never been to Sacramento, but you get the point.)

After I'd spent a few days feeling guilty and annoyed that I possess such an innate ability to be awful, Augie came over to my house and we spent our second night together. We got romantically stoned, and I showed him around the very haunted house I was living in. The house belonged to my friend Eric Gilliland, who had purchased it in the late eighties when twentysomethings could become bajillionaires for writing multi-cam sitcom pilots in their spare time that would never see the light of day while running popular shows that tens of millions of people tuned in for every week. Eric had relocated to New York in the 2000s after a huge showrunning career but had held on to his beautiful cabin right outside Beverly Hills, a cabin that hadn't been touched since it was built in 1934 by the silent movie superstar Buster Keaton. The legend was that Buster had built the place for his new wife in the midst of what was his career low point. Having been forced out of the limelight by talking pictures, he spent most of those days getting drunk and playing cards with Fatty Arbuckle (the movie star who a now-debunked urban legend used to claim went to prison for an act of horrific and fatal sexual assault that you can read all about in *Hollywood Babylon* if you are in the mood to puke all over yourself). While my career had barely existed, it was most certainly at an all-time low, so Buster's historically depressive haze hanging over the house was a perfect fit for me and my despondent wondering that maybe my dreams were never coming true after all.

This place was comically haunted. After all, it was built by one of our greatest clowns. Faucets turned on by themselves, doors suddenly slammed then opened again, furniture got rearranged in the middle of the night, a music box without batteries would suddenly begin playing music, and countless nights I awoke to the sight of a man standing at the foot of the bed.

I knew about the house's spooky history when I moved in and was more than a little nervous about living in a haunted house. However, Eric wasn't charging me rent, and few things can get a person over their fears more quickly than a free two-bedroom house in Los Angeles with a huge backyard and a working fireplace.

I had moved into the house with my ex-boyfriend Patrick, and when he left, I was even more petrified to live there alone. My first solo night in the house, I sat down in the middle of the floor and spoke aloud to the ghost like (depending on how you look at it) an unhinged lunatic or a spiritually evolved person in chunky turquoise jewelry. I told the ghost how scared I was to live there alone and how I'd never lived anywhere alone before, and then I asked if we could be kind to each other. I would respect their ghostly life if they respected my (debatably) mortal one. I told them how brokenhearted I was and that I hoped to someday find a new person to live there with and when that day came, I hoped the ghost would be my friend and give me a sign that the person should stick around. (These are the type of conversations a person living in LA too long starts to have. You should have heard the ones I was having with my ottoman.)

After a couple of years living in the house alone, I felt a kinship with the ghost. I'd been through the breakup but also an endless array of unsuccessful auditions, unpurchased TV show pitches, and failed staff writing interviews. I felt lost at the unknown sea of rejection that's the only moisture in that glorious and awful desert of a city. But I always felt proud that what used to scare me about the house had become a weird sort of comfort. Then, the morning after Augie had slept over for the first time, he was taking a shower when suddenly he felt his hair jerked as if by someone standing behind him. When he came out of the shower, soaking wet and looking terrified, I first thought, *Um, hot*. But then second, I remembered my conversation with the ghost and realized they had just given me the sign I had asked for all those years before. Again, LA does a lot to a person's mind.

Augie was fresh off an HBO Mike White pilot that had sadly not been picked up, was crazy broke, and was on the verge of losing his apartment downtown. We spent pretty much every night of our first four weeks together in that sun-filled loft. It was a beautiful space, but he had never put up curtains and not only did the exposure wake one up at the butt crack of dawn, but one day (after some other butt crack business) we awoke to a sign in a neighbor's window reading, "CURTAINS, PLEASE!" Augie moved into the haunted house the next day.

We entered into our domesticity fast and furiously. Everything was perfect in that way that things are in the early days of a relationship when it feels as though nothing could possibly come between the two of you. Our first fight wasn't so much a fight as it was me having a full-blown hallucinogenic manic episode at a backyard party where I became convinced that a fiftysomething woman named Paige who we randomly met among the party guests was having a top-secret affair with Augie. I went absolutely nuts and stormed out of the party, much to Augie's utter shock and disbelief.

His confusion was made even worse by the fact that I had not told Augie about my—let's call it "colorful"—mental health. Also, in the excitement of our budding love I had done what I often do in moments of unexpected bliss: I stopped taking my meds. A medication vacation, I like to call it in an attempt to turn the toxic into the "adorkable." The unhealthy logic is that I do this to truly feel joy in its shiny new form without any medicinal filter, but inevitably all that ends up happening is a couple of days of manic euphoria before things start to teeter closer and closer to madness. That teeter hit its totter at that backyard party, and the look on Augie's face as he chased after me down the driveway brought me back to whatever version of earth it is I occupy.

After he assured me that, no, he was not having a secret affair with the woman we had just met at the drinks table, he asked me what was really going on. I admitted the thing I had been avoiding admitting, that I have to take a handful of medication twice a day in order not to rip my own face off while jumping off the Hollywood Sign.

He was completely unfazed and has remained the same ever since. This is obviously not an easy position to take during an earthquake in the snow globe of my psychosis, but still Augie somehow weathers the constant flakes of the mentally unpredictable that never seem to stop swirling around me. He never ceases to surprise me in his ability to forgive and wrap his head around the hurly-burly mayhem that is me.

At some point after our first few years together, he took me back up that same mountain in Altadena, asked me if I was hungry, and handed me an orange from his backpack. I peeled it, only to find what appeared to be a gross-looking piece of metal inside, before turning around to find him beaming up at me from one knee, where he asked, "Well, what do you think?"

I said yes, then we sat in our spot, with our very own oranges and their peels while we drank a room-temp bottle of Dom Pérignon from his backpack.

It didn't take long for married life to reveal itself as far more complicated and messy than it appears on the surface. Even when you're two nonmonogamous men going to weekly therapy, with very independent lives, marriage remains a sandbox of roses and razor blades. When you live with someone so intimately, with not just your hearts tied up together but your logistical lives as well, it's not long before that person becomes a sort of mirror . . . a mirror for all the bullshit you call your everyday behavior. Over time, with each jab or fight or deceit, that mirror cracks just a little bit more, but it keeps doing its job because a cracked mirror is still a mirror, like George and Martha in *Who's Afraid of Virginia Woolf?*, who reflect the good and terrible about each other every day, over and over, past two intermissions if you're watching the play. It's what makes me constantly wonder, *Why am I married?*

It often feels like it could be much easier, that I could get away with my worst qualities in a much smoother fashion, if there was no one there to witness them so reliably. And because Augie and I are often locationally separated for work, I frequently get the opportunity to try single life on for size. To see just how well or how terribly it fits to have no true intimacy or accountability or partner to steal the duvet.

The biggest version of this occurred at the tail end of 2020 (that easy breezy CoverGirl of a year). Augie was filming the television series of *Lord of the Rings* in New Zealand. Like everything else, it had gotten shut down for COVID, but unlike most everything else, they were back and running by summer. He stepped back into the old-school reality that New Zealand had maintained due to its intense border control and quarantine mandates, while I was stuck in LA just as we were getting our first brush with those now familiar words "surge" and "variant." Around this time, I had dug myself out of yet another financial and creative hole by selling a scripted miniseries to Quibi (just when you thought this story couldn't get more 2020). It was a super-duper high-concept project directly from my heart and my very stoned brain, and within weeks of pitching it, I was meeting with animators and studios and having all the other Zoom meetings a person needed to feel the 2020 version of thriving. Everyone involved and in my orbit was encouraging enough for me to believe that I was finally getting to make the unhinged comedy epic I'd always wanted to make. AND that I would get paid!

Meanwhile, Augie was in an enviable groove in New Zealand in the unique way that actors on location get into; because of the time difference and my newfound obsession with my big, exciting project, our communication got more and more strained. Then, a few weeks into preproduction planning, I (like so many other people high on the questionably alluring prospect of creating five-minute episodic content to be viewed on a phone) awoke to read that Quibi was officially dead.

The distance from Augie, the isolation of COVID, the impending doom of the presidential election, and the high and now low of the Quibi project created a perfect storm, and I dove headfirst into one of the deepest depressions I've ever had. I started sleeping pretty much all day every day, avoiding interaction with anyone whatsoever. I got up to walk the dog before going back to sleep, then spent the evenings drinking at least one bottle of wine while staying up all night taking bumps of cocaine on my own while watching every Tony Awards telecast I could find on YouTube going back to 1981. For those of you considering trying this at home, maybe don't. But if you must, don't try to watch past 1981. Yes, there are recordings of the seventies telecasts, but once you get into the seventies, the quality is too fuzzy and hazy. Much like the seventies themselves and, at that time, my own brain.

Believe it or not, doing drugs and drinking alone for a month or so without seeing anyone didn't help my depression and made everything far, far worse. By the end of the month, not only was I being a Dairy Queen cold bitch to Augie the few times a week that I'd answer his calls, but I was also busy making half-assed attempts to kill myself. Nothing concrete, just flirting with the prospect of annihilation without going all the way. I was Sandy in *Grease* necking with Danny but not letting him get to second base despite his pleading, or rather I was not actually slicing my wrists but casually dragging our sharpest kitchen knife over them while I watched Christine Baranski accept her 1984 Tony Award for *The Real Thing* while I cried, did coke, and tried to talk myself into going all the way. If you've seen my screen work, I am sure you can agree that I am never short of on the nose. Coke or not.

Finally, I pushed Augie completely away. I was in full self-sabotage mode, and much like the nightly drug use and knife play, I wanted to push my marriage as far as I could without actually breaking skin. But finally, I did. I broke it. (Us, not my wrists. They remain slender and fine.) Augie called after one particularly chaotically furious and incoherent conversation on my part to say he couldn't do it anymore; he couldn't take the shit I was hurling at him, the unpredictability, and he couldn't keep trying to help me get it together while I refused to even talk to him.

I sobbed gutturally for a few hours before I took a Klonopin, slept a lot, and woke up the next morning to find a therapist for the first time in a decade. I knew I'd royally fucked up, and everyone around me knew it too. I wrote out my game plan, took a shower for the first time in what can't have been less than ten days, and eventually called Augie to read a two-page manifesto about how I was going to turn my personal *Titanic* around before it hit the forecasted iceberg made of cocaine and destruction straight ahead.

Augie did what has slowly and with lots of mutual work become a pattern in our marriage: he listened. He took in all the ramblings of my refried bean brain and mutterings from what has medically been declared my heart. He told me that I was welcome to take the trip to New Zealand that had been planned for Christmas to see him and reconnect face-to-face after the four months we'd now spent apart . . . but that he couldn't promise me anything. I'd really hurt him in the past months, not just by being Bond villain–caliber vicious the few times I'd pick up his call but also by not cluing him in to all the garbage that had been going on with me at home.

I hadn't let in anyone, but especially not the person I was supposed to have committed to always telling the truth to, the person who had become my mirror. If I'd done that, though, I would've had to face my own truth, and well, that was simply not something I wanted to deal with. Besides, I hadn't even finished my eight ball of blow or gotten to the 1997 Tony Awards telecast yet! Folks, that's when Rosie started hosting, and this was *really* good coke!

As things shifted, it was planned that I'd go see Augie in New Zealand after all, maybe to reconnect or maybe to consciously uncouple on the other side of the world. The moment I hung up our call, I jumped into my car and started driving cross-country to Georgia, where I planned to leave our dog Cheech with my folks while I was on the trip that I had consistently put off all fall, to hopefully save my marriage to a man currently playing an elf on the other side of the world. I also knew that if I stayed home alone any longer, I would run out of Tony Award clips and probably lose a nostril too.

After a healing week in Georgia, I flew to New Zealand, where I had to immediately enter a full-fledged fourteen-day government-run quarantine. I was installed at a hotel surrounded by barbed-wire fencing near the airport where military people with literal machine guns guarded the gates, making sure no one came in and no one got out. I was stuck there in a room with a view of a parking lot where we were permitted to walk around in circles during daylight hours for as long as we wanted. As if the vibe weren't apocalyptic enough, the hotel was across the street from an amusement park that had seen better days. It wasn't long before I got weed brownies smuggled in (and I'm not saying how). So for those two weeks, my everyday routine involved ingesting mediocre weed before standing outside in the parking lot and listening to the sounds of spooky carnival music and screaming children across a barbed-wire fence.

Once I was finally out and reconnected with Augie, it wasn't the immediate smooth sailing I was hoping it would be. There were still so many frustrating walls that I had erected myself and so many wounds that I'd sliced open with my own manic and cruel tongue. The first couple of weeks were bumpy, as if we were strangers who also happened to know every awful thing about each other. We eventually took off on a road trip because if you're going to have an awkward time with your spouse during the holidays, it might as well be through the South Island of New Zealand during a tourism drought because of a global pandemic that ensures you discounted five-star properties in nearly abandoned beach towns.

Over our three-week road trip, the vibe was the type that you'd expect between a married couple whose relationship has recently almost ended due to one of them being a drug-abusing maniac toying with suicide who claims something called Quibi as an excuse for his insanity. We took a train ride through the New Zealand Alps, where I got testy over Augie wanting to befriend the two other passengers in the first-class cabin, and where I got upset over the lack of Christmas decorations everywhere we went because, like Joel's Australia, in New Zealand Christmas is in summer and who wants to see a Santa hat in ninety-degree weather? (Me, by the way. If it's after November first, put up some twinkle lights or get the fuck out of my face.) We both continued to struggle with our own resentments toward each other and the weirdness of being in the same bed again. The radio was singing that it was a holly jolly marshmallow world, but ours most certainly wasn't.

Finally, one day we were in a village called Punakaiki, where we went to the local pub after some sort of heated debate over our future while settling into our "bach" (a little beach shack) that had been built over a hundred years before. While Augie and I were completely out of sync, the village of Punakaiki itself was just as unsyncopated. The tiny village is usually a tourist hot spot during the holiday season, but this year brought no visitors as there were no international tourists and the locals were staying home. The sole local pub was so empty that we helped the elderly woman running the place bring in the outdoor furniture before she shut down for the week due to the lack of business. While we did so, Augie asked her about any hidden things to see nearby that aren't in the tourist books, and her eyes lit up. She explained that just off the highway was a cave that was very popular with tourists. However, she explained, if you go off the marked path within the cave and follow a very complicated set of directions further down, you could find a cavern covered in glowworms. Augie could not have been more into this idea, but I protested, reminding him of my intense fear of snakes and activity in general. I thought I had gotten out of the outing without further marriage conflict, but then the elderly pub owner retorted, "There's nothing in New Zealand that can kill you." Bitch.

Later that night, when Augie emerged from our bach carrying two flashlights and a spliff and announced we were taking the pub owner's cave advice, I fumed but bit my tongue. I'd done enough damage the previous few months, and if trekking into a cave in the middle of the night in search of glowworms could bring some sort of joy to our highly stilted vibe, it was probably my duty to do it.

We trekked through the pitch-black cave, stepping into murky puddles, the air getting colder and colder the deeper into the cave we went, and I despised every moment of it. Finally, we crawled through a rock tunnel that simply screamed, "Hey, girl! This is where you'll die," and entered into a cavern so small we had to lie down. And that's where, with our backs to the slimy stone somewhere beneath the earth's surface on a continent nowhere near anything I'd ever known, we turned off our flashlights and found the entire cave so covered in glowworms that we might as well have been lit by klieg lights outside of Grauman's Chinese Theatre the night *Who's Afraid of Virginia Woolf?* premiered.

There's no way not to be cliché here, but it was mesmerizing. Sure, they sorta looked like snakes that had been to a rave and swallowed glow sticks and enough ketamine to keep themselves motionless, but if I didn't think about that too hard, they were simply lamps, and who doesn't love a lamp? (Besides the mom in *A Christmas Story*, and wasn't this my Christmas story?) We lay there, lit in this prehistoric lighting, and we kissed for a very long time, staring into each other's eyes. The light of the worms hit our irises just right, making our eyeballs mirrors of each other. Just like those same mirrors that crack and shatter with each tiny hurt that a couple becomes to each other. The same mirrors made of pieces you constantly figure out new ways to put back together, a constantly shifting puzzle called togetherness. No matter how many dents and cracks a mirror gets, it still finds new ways to reflect not just you but the light and the darkness as well—all the things that bring you joy and make you laugh, but also the things that you're most afraid of. Maybe it's the unknown or your own untrustworthy brain or your self-annihilating tendencies, or maybe it's just Virginia Woolf.

But you're afraid and you're hopeful and you're growing up.

Together.

And I guess that's it? That's why. That's marriage.

# Final Ten Reasons Not to Sabotage Your Life

1. The joy of someone canceling plans so you don't have to.
2. Passing a jack-o'-lantern with lit candles inside it while on an evening stroll on a night that's cool enough to need a jacket but warm enough not to need a coat.
3. Spending an entire evening watching every possible version of Sondheim's "I'm Still Here" on YouTube. (You'll need at least five hours, A LOT of wine, and some patience for Betty Garrett.)
4. The pride of not needing a map in Manhattan.
5. Videos of rescue pigs having great lives.
6. Filling your backpack with stolen snacks from a film set craft services table.
7. Hooking up with strangers in the Equinox steam room.
8. Anytime you run into Ellen Barkin walking her dog in your neighborhood while you're walking your

own dog. While the dogs ecstatically play, you try to come up with the cleverest thing to say in your bid to get Ellen Barkin to become your best friend, inevitably giving up and choosing instead to just play it cool, walking away grateful you didn't embarrass yourself—yet.

9. Finding the perfect public bathroom when you really, really have to go.
10. Tomorrow. And the next day. And the next one. And the next . . .

# Run and Hide

There was this girl in one of the tap dance classes I took as a kid who was a fucking star. I and two other boys were the only male students at the local dance studio, and because of this fact we were featured in more dance numbers than anyone else in the yearly recital. It was the nineties, and even at a girls' after-school dance academy men had a leg up (and not just in the kick line). But this girl—let's call her Lulu because that wasn't her name and I don't know anyone named that (thank God)—was really, really good, but she was always forced behind me and the other boys because of the unspoken gendered hierarchy. As the years went on, the other two boys grew into preteens who understood that a weekly rehearsal spent shuffling off to Buffalo to the Andrew Sisters' rendition of "Boogie Woogie Bugle Boy" was not the type of thing you carve out time for when you are a seventh-grade boy. At least, not if you want friends. This notion, however, was completely lost on me, and I continued twirling and tapping as my image slowly morphed from adorable little boy to flaming gay guy. Being the last man standing in the dance school led to my being featured in even more numbers every year. Me center stage belting out *Singin' in the Rain* while the girls Maxie Ford-ed behind me? Yep. Me dressed as early eighties Michael Jackson complete with solo silver glove and the type of problematic jerry curl wig a person could write a three-thousand-word think piece about? But of course!

I wasn't very good, I was just the boy, and this did not make me the most popular kid at the dance studio, especially not with that girl, Lulu, who was a fucking star. While she mostly ignored me with a smoldering menace, her mother was incapable of camouflaging what can only be described as utter disdain.

This was disorienting because usually moms were my thing. I had grown up with a perfect blond bowl cut, innocent blue eyes, and a mischievous smile so adorable I could've been a Culkin. Usually, I could melt the heart of even the most uptight mom or teacher—but not this lady, not Lulu's mom. Lulu's mom had the type of cocky air about her that you can only have if you look down on everything in the world that isn't your daughter or the Olympic-size Styrofoam cup of sweet tea that this woman seemed to keep attached to her person at all times. Lulu's mom was a grown-up mean girl who'd successfully cornered her clique of sycophantic other moms, a gaggle of shit-talking bullies doused in fruity perfumes purchased at Merle Norman and haircuts serving up Laura Bush cosplay. It was their years of tuition that kept the school's lights on, so this was their territory to rule, their little corner of the world in which to decide who got to fit in and who got to suffer. If you became their target, you were toast, and as I became featured more and more in each dance recital that passed, I became crisp and ready to be buttered. I'd see Lulu's mom looking at me and whispering to one of her sidekicks and know I was done for.

As I grew from kid to preteen, I was sure she'd spotted one of my naturally limp-wristed gesticulations, which I was quickly learning were disgustingly flamboyant, effeminate, and wrong. It wasn't long before she became an ice-cold wall between my progressively lonelier self and everyone else in the dance class. I tried to convince myself it was something else entirely that she so clearly hated about me. Maybe she had a thing against natural blonds? Lord knows the bleached blond rat's nest atop her own head wasn't natural.

Or maybe she was mad I wasn't in *more* dance numbers? I didn't take ballet class, so those dances were boy-less. Maybe she wasn't staring at me with a seething distaste but was actually fuming over the fact that I wasn't arabesque-ing with the girls to "Just Around the Riverbend" from Disney's *Pocahontas*. (All of the girls were dressed in spandex bastardizations of Native American attire, by the way. Dance recitals in the nineties served as vaudevilles of cancelable offenses.)

Or maybe she was jealous of me? She had a sexy husband, a Patrick Dempsey type who often picked up his daughter from dance practice in a T-shirt that hugged his perfectly defined pecs. Even at eleven years old, I imagined sipping daiquiris with him by a Palm Springs pool. I tried to tell myself that the reason Lulu's mom so clearly disliked me had nothing to do with the way I presented myself but was based solely on the fact that she could sense my feelings for her husband so she was jealously threatened. Reminder: I was eleven.

As the years passed with more dance recitals centered around me, puberty started to hit me like Halley's Homosexual Comet. Everything about me got gayer (and it's not like we were dealing with John Wayne beforehand). As I grew, it all went the wrong way. My voice changed from that of an innocent child to that of an opinionated interior decorator wearing an ascot. My thick bouncy hair was adorable on a little boy, but on a dandy preteen it looked more like Julie Andrews in *The Sound of Music*. Overnight I went from a precocious prince to a preening poofter, and there was absolutely nothing I could do to hide it. Certainly not while tap dancing on a suitcase to "Fascinating Rhythm," which I did as a solo for one year's opening number . . . knowing full well even then that it was hardly interesting, let alone fascinating.

During a dance recital after my pubescent ascent into queenliness, I was walking backstage, hair spray and asbestos filling the air. Because of my being the only boy, I had my own dressing room right outside the one for everyone else. I could overhear the moms having a conversation in the type of hushed tone that meant they were shit-talking, so obviously I stopped and hid behind the doorframe to snoop.

Sure enough, it was Lulu's mom leading an informal board meeting with her equally vicious maternal minions.

"Well, it just makes me uncomfortable," one of the moms was saying.

"Me too," another added. "It's not safe for him to be around our girls."

I had the sinking suspicion that the "he" in question was me, seeing as I was the only guy backstage, and this was proven correct when Lulu's mom declared to her loyal subjects, "It's bad enough they put the little faggot in every number."

This little folksy token of affection was met by stifled laughter from Lulu's mom's coven of Karens as they cackled around their nonexistent cauldron.

"He isn't even a good dancer," she added, putting the cherry atop my budding sundae of fury.

I was standing on the cement steps leading down to the basement dressing room at the town auditorium. I was wearing a Reba-at-the-CMAs level of makeup; tap shoes that I was quickly outgrowing; and a glittery red, white, and blue tuxedo made out of 100 percent flammable materials. I looked like Joel Grey in *Cabaret* as produced by the Proud Boys. I was thirteen and so humiliated I felt it from my toes up to my head, where a sequin-covered top hat was perched atop my hair, which was too voluminous for a boy.

I was momentarily frozen on the outside while inside my entire being coursed with the red-hot heat it takes decades to identify as shame and not certain death. I felt not just like a freak but also like I was in enormous trouble, that I had done something terribly wrong, that the Mary Kay red on my cheeks was actually from the blood on my hands.

It wasn't long, however, before my sizzling shame transformed to unhinged anger. I wanted to bound down the stairs to Lulu's mother and her nasty little crew of Talbots-clad wannabes and rip them to shreds with the type of operatic monologue that would make even Julia Sugarbaker blush:

"First of all, welcome to the faggot-tastic world of dance, honey. Sit down at your computer, ask fucking Jeeves to name some famous gay choreographers, and pack a lunch! Second of all, be logical! Wouldn't you rather my sparkly gay ass over the type of leering straight boys at school who are sure to knock your daughters up by the time they're sixteen? And third of all"—this part would've been directed at Lulu's mom—"It's your hot husband inside my spank bank, and he could do a damn lot better than your ugly Channel Five weather lady haircut ass!"

But I was thirteen, so hurt it scared me, and confused that grown-ups could be that cruel to someone who wasn't even their own kid. So instead of launching into my tirade, I ran to the bathroom and cried my makeup off, hiding until it was time to go back onstage to dance in my stupid costume, realizing that the parts of myself I tried so desperately to see as "special" were simply bad and unacceptable to other people. I was a guilty freak whose evolution into the type of adult one is supposed to avoid had already begun, and there was no stopping it. I wanted to hide and never, ever be found.

And that, I suppose, is a common event in this book. No, not just stupid costumes and the desire to rip someone to shreds in the style of Dixie Carter's iconic character from *Designing Women*, but also running away from the seascape of shame that I always seem to be looking out over from my sun lounger of self-pity at the all-inclusive resort of my self-esteem. That shame has been my constant copilot while writing this book. Some days he can show up just to give me a quick "Hey girl," as if he worries I'll forget him if I go too long without his wrath. Or he can arrive with no return ticket, an air mattress for my living room, and a stack of luggage so excessive it includes a hatbox. Once moved in for his indeterminate stay, he will make himself more than at home. He'll put the thermostat on eighty if I want it on seventy, he'll drain the Brita and never refill it, he'll track mud and shit and hate all over the floors, and he'll keep me up all night pounding pots and pans inside my already noising brain.

And that shame is what I find myself constantly running away and hiding from. Over and over and over. Anytime I am faced with conflict, pain, my manic lows, or even mere discomfort with reality, I run and hide. Whether it's to a bathroom stall away from hurt feelings or under my covers for days on end, I am always ready to bolt to the nearest shadowy corner where no one can find me for as long as I can stay hidden. I can't, however, blame Lulu's mom or anyone else from that embarrassing day at the dance recital for this. I was running away and hiding long before that. It has never not been my second nature.

My earliest Steve McQueen–style great escapes into obscurity usually followed some sort of fight with my parents where I felt like I was in trouble: baby shame. I'd grab a bag, say my goodbyes, then hit the road like a drifter off to see the world, with such a lot of world to see, off to find a moon river for you and for me. I'd make my sad stroll down the driveway very, very slowly, even slower than Dolly Levi descending the stairs into Harmonia Gardens in *Hello, Dolly!* (which is extremely slow, by the way). If Dolly is so glad to be back where she belongs that she can sing an entire number and encore about it, then maybe just get to your seat and order, babe? People are trying to eat their goose and dumplings, but now you've got every waiter in the joint quite literally galloping. *Hello, Dolly!*? More like *Hurry the Fuck Up, Dolly!*

But maybe Dolly was trying to be stopped, to be told to turn back. I know I certainly was on my pilgrimages into the unpredictable territory of being a six-year-old hitchhiker. Who's to say how it would have ended up for my childhood self if I had actually run away and never come back, but it's safe to guess: terribly. Needless to say, I never made it very far. Just across the street to a slightly wooded area where I could feel far enough away that I felt like I'd run where nobody and no problems could find me . . . but still close enough to come back if my mom panicked and started searching for me. After the third or fourth time in a week, she didn't.

After a while I'd just keep my bag packed with the belongings I needed to run away with. Those included Little Debbie oatmeal pies, a towel, a change of clothes, and a copy of the collected plays of Neil Simon, volume two. No specific reason for that particular volume, other than the fact that it was the only one I had purchased at the library's used book sale. Hey, I may have been furious enough to run away, but I was eventually going to improve my reading skills enough to devour *The Prisoner of Second Avenue*, dammit. Usually after an hour I'd get bored enough to go home and pretend none of it had happened, asking, "What *is* for dinner anyway?"

This routine became the norm, and after a while it seemed like I should be paying property taxes for that wooded area across the street. But no one tried to stop it, probably because on the list of the most annoying things about having to live with me, "him running away to hide behind a tree across the street, pretend to read, look needy, and leave us the fuck alone for an hour" was likely pretty low.

This beginning of this intoxicating instinct to run and hide from uncomfortable feelings opened up a world of avoidance that would soon become the place I most consider home. Whether to the sickroom at school, behind the bleachers, a paint closet at the community theater, under my bed . . . big uncomfortable feelings always equaled the same pattern.

The summer after my sixth-grade year, a professional theater company came to my hometown direct from New York City. The person who'd started the company had grown up in town and was bringing down a crew of her college friends, and other actors hired in New York, to do a "summer stock" season of plays and musicals. My mom noticed an ad in the paper encouraging locals of all ages to audition for chorus roles. They were putting on *As You Like It*, *The Pirates of Penzance*, and *She Loves Me*—and this Stage Door Nelly was READY.

When my mom brought me to the Saturday auditions, we discovered I was the only person in the entire town who'd shown up. Despite the fact that none of the three shows had characters in them that screamed "child actor," the director could tell just how intensely I wanted to be any part of this whatsoever. They very generously found me small roles in every show they put on that summer: a child page in the Shakespeare, a child pirate in the Gilbert and Sullivan, and a child busboy in *She Loves Me*. All in all, a pretty thorough tour de force of child labor practices throughout the ages.

The entire company of professional actors lived in dorms on the college campus that happened to be directly across the street from our house, and I basically never let these twentysomething thespians out of my sight. I was obsessed with each and every one of them. By this time, I was a walking encyclopedia of musical theater trivia, which had never been met by anything but sneers and jeers from my peers. Now, for the first time, I was around people who hadn't just heard of Stephen Sondheim, they'd heard of Stephen Schwartz as well and knew that Sondheim was better. Despite how terribly annoying I must have been, they took me in, encouraged me, laughed at my jokes, and gave me all the attention I so deeply craved, which (as you can probably guess at this point in this solo circle jerk of ego captured in personal essays) is A LOT of attention. They were the first people not just to see and accept me for being me but to celebrate it too.

Like all great summers, though, this one eventually came to an end, and it was the most devastated I had ever been in my entire thirteen years of life. The circus was leaving town, and all I wanted was to hide in the box of gaffer tape and wigs. My parents dropped me off at the company's farewell dinner, but as I walked in, the weight of saying goodbye to these kindred spirits became so overwhelming that I hid in a bathroom stall for the entire hour without going into the party until it was time for me to get picked up. I couldn't fathom a farewell, so I did what I knew to do: I hid.

Two years later, I ran away into one of my longest periods of hiding. Luckily, I didn't have far to run. I was finishing eighth grade at the small Catholic school I had attended since I was five with the dreaded next step of entering high school looming ahead like the check at the end of a fancy dinner where you've ordered the "market price" fish but didn't check the cost because you wanted to seem rich. I knew if middle schoolers had been tough on me as they began to realize just how different from them I was, then teenagers were going to be a total nightmare.

My two options for ninth grade were either a very stuffy private school in town that we couldn't afford and that I didn't get into anyway or the local public school with thousands and thousands of students. I panicked and began obsessively researching alternatives, becoming increasingly dead set on figuring out a way to skip the four-year period of high school entirely and jump straight ahead to life as an early twentysomething in New York City.

I found a four-year online high school program based out of Ojai, California, where teachers put together a year's worth of lesson plans in each subject and the students worked at their own pace from the comfort of their home. Nowadays, this doesn't sound that bizarre, but in 2001 it was met by the type of raised eyebrows pretty much everything else I did received. But it wasn't hard to convince my parents to go along with it, so with a dial-up connection, a Jurassic-era HTML website, and pajama pants I rarely changed out of, I managed to run away from everything I feared about high school and hide in the safety of my bedroom before I even had to start.

For my next trick, I ran again, but this time not to hide but instead to go to New York at the questionable age of seventeen and work as an assistant to a Tony Award–winning director on Broadway.

As I would eventually do with Gary Beach, I had sent a fan letter to a Broadway stage door. This particular letter, the first I'd ever sent, was for Joe Mantello, who had recently won the Tony Award for directing *Take Me Out*, a play about a closeted baseball player that (important to my gay teen soul) featured shower scenes with chiseled actors doing full frontal nudity. Oh yeah, I also really loved the play. At the time, I wanted to be a theater director when I grew up, and upon a deep dive of Joe's illustrious career, I discovered he wasn't just very talented; he was also a key figure in all things modern gay theater history. He had starred in the original production of *Angels in America*, he had directed a boatload of original Terrence McNally plays, and he was currently directing a new musical about the Wicked Witch of the West called *Wicked*. Pretty fucking gay. I wrote him a heartfelt letter about how much I had loved his play, about my dreams of being a director, and audaciously about the community theater company I'd started in my hometown. If I had access to that self-congratulatory letter today, I would likely either vomit from reading it or eat the piece of paper to avoid having to read it at all (and then vomit it). Joe sweetly replied (from tech rehearsals of the first Broadway production of Sondheim's *Assassins*, no less) giving me his email address, to which I obviously wrote.

We slowly developed a pen-pal relationship. Him, a multi-award-winning director at the top of his game, and me, a very lonely gay kid in a small southern town who was homeschooling himself and hiding from the real life of being a teenager at all costs. Maybe he could sense my loneliness, or maybe he was just nice and bored. Regardless, he started to turn my longing imaginations of what life in New York might be into a reality. I got a momentary rush anytime my computer announced, "You've got mail," and I'd rush to see if it was from him.

After a year or so of me emailing updates on all my community projects, Joe invited me to be his personal assistant on a show he was directing. My parents were, as usual, confused enough to be aggressively supportive, so they let me go stay with a friend I'd made from that visiting summer theater company. And just when you thought this book couldn't get gayer: I arrived in New York to be Joe Mantello's personal assistant as he directed Mario Cantone's one-man Broadway show called *Laugh Whore*. That sentence alone should get this book on some GLAAD list and then promptly banned in some states.

The plan I had made with my parents was that after the show opened and my job ended, I would return home and to normal life, but the minute I got to New York and saw everything that came with it, there was absolutely no way I was going back home. The only thing that seemed easier than running away was running away while I was already gone. So I told my parents I had been hired for another assistant job and promised I'd come home after that one. They accepted this with their usual support, but the issue was that there was no next job. I had nothing lined up, no correspondence with other Broadway directors, and no clue how to find the next gig that I had allegedly already booked.

With the nauseating prospect of having to go back to the

humdrum of my real life, I experienced the same tenacious commitment to finding what to do next that I'd felt when figuring out how to hide from high school. I didn't know how, but I knew I had to keep running while I was already lapping the track. I scoured the job listings on Playbill.com like it was the only thing standing between me and death, which is how I eventually ended up with my next assistant-to-a-director job. The gig with Joe had paid, but this new one was an unpaid internship assisting an elderly director named Melvin Bernhardt. He had once been a successful Broadway and television director but was now directing a pretty terrible play called *Texas Homos* at a small theater in an office building near Penn Station. Melvin wasn't particularly nice, and his vision (both optically and creatively) had seen better days. But I didn't care. I got to sit in a black-box theater pretending to scribble on a yellow legal pad while I watched him and the brilliant actor Reed Birney scream each other's heads off. Melvin had spent too many decades directing daytime soap operas and had forgotten how to navigate the feelings of actors, and as far as feelings go, Reed had plenty. Years later, Reed Birney won a Tony for his fantastic performance in *The Humans* (directed by Joe Mantello), and Melvin Bernhardt died (not directed by Joe Mantello).

Without ever saying so out loud to anyone, including myself, I had decided I was never going back home ever again. Sure, I didn't have any income. Sure, I was still crashing at a friend's apartment and avoiding answering the question of "When are you leaving?" Sure, I was still "in" high school, but I'd already run to the place I had always planned on running to. And now I was there hiding from the reality I'd left back home. This wasn't running away with a duffel bag of things to a tree across the street only to turn around and come home for dinner. This time, there was no turning back.

After *Texas Homos* opened, I had to find my next job, and once again I told my parents that I had already found it. I desperately tracked down a few interviews for jobs I didn't get. The last interview I had was to intern for a director named John Tillinger, who had directed lots of very successful Broadway shows. While Joe had been so supportive and kind, John was even less enthused by me than Melvin Bernhardt had been. John was dismissive, condescending, and unkind as I sat across from him in a conference room at the offices of Manhattan Theatre Club. He had a smug, demoralizing condescension and treated me as exactly what I knew I was: a nobody kid who knew nothing from a small town no one had ever heard of who had absolutely zero business being in New York. He sucked up all the unfounded confidence and bubbling ambition I had spilling out of me at that point, and he spit it out into an office water fountain underneath a framed poster for *The Tale of the Allergist's Wife*. I left the office, tail between my legs, with the feeling of professional rejection that I had, at this point in my life, only felt once before when I was fired from the Barnes & Noble Cafe for always forgetting to ask people to sign credit card receipts. But that moment of rejection had been easy. Sure, I was losing my Barnes & Noble discount, but with this snooty director I felt I was losing the entirety of my dreams.

Lost in the type of "you will never make it" haze I would learn to wake up with every day for the rest of my life, I wandered up

Eighth Avenue, questioning whether I should've just gone home when I'd originally planned to, which is when a very large and intimidating man bumped into me. He let out a shout as he dropped a glass bottle in a paper bag. It shattered everywhere. He immediately became enraged, screaming that it was a one-hundred-dollar bottle of wine, then pinned me against a wall on the corner of Eighth Avenue and Forty-Eighth Street, demanding I give him money. I froze, never having been as terrified in my life.

I calmly pleaded for him to stop, to leave me alone, explaining I had no cash. But when he picked up a sharp shard of broken glass, I agreed to go inside a nearby deli and get money out of the ATM for him.

Trembling, I got the cash with this aggressive creep towering over me. I knew I was getting swindled. I should've asked for help, I should've jumped into a cab, I should've known that the bottle was empty and that this was a hoax to get someone like me to give him money, that this was an occasion to *actually* run away and hide . . . but instead, I got out the cash, handed it to him, and he left. The next day I flew back to Georgia scared shitless, dreams stomped, realizing I wasn't as grown up as I so desperately wanted to be. Disappointed with myself, I ran back home and hid after thinking I'd run away for good.

Back in Georgia, I was depressed over the fact that I'd tried running away to New York only to turn around and run away from that. Now I faced the pesky realization that I had no clue what I was supposed to do with the rest of my life. *And* I was only seventeen. I had always thought things would all work out in New York. My fairy-tale ending always revolved around a 212 area code (and in dire straits, 917). Now I was back in my childhood bed having my first dance at the Realization Some Things Aren't Meant to Be Ball, where I didn't just leave my glass slipper but all my confidence as well.

I sat around, watched so many old movies TCM should've paid me, allegedly finished "high school," and felt bad for myself so long that I decided I had to do something. I decided to bite the bullet, try to be a normal kid, and go to college. The very notion felt cliché. Shopping for dorm room furniture? Declaring a major? Waking up in the morning? Yuck. But I felt I'd tried enough alternative routes that maybe a little old-fashioned structure would do me good. Plus, it was a new place to run away and hide.

Joe had gone to the University of North Carolina School of the Arts, which happened to have a program for theater directing, so at the last minute I applied there. I can't imagine my application was what one might call alluring, what with the whole "no real high school education whatsoever" thing. Also, I'd hastily taken my SATs the year prior but was so preoccupied directing an evening of Christopher Durang short plays (you can imagine how big a hit those were in Rome, Georgia) that I just colored in circles at random instead of actually reading the test. I don't know what the score ended up being, but I do remember it made people giggle whenever I revealed it. Regardless, though, none of that ended up mattering because I did a decent enough audition monologue and Joe wrote me a very kind recommendation letter. I was one of the thirty students accepted into the drama division. This was all under the school's condition that I wouldn't receive an actual BFA (I cannot stress enough just how bad those SAT scores were). Unlike everyone else in my class, I'd simply get "an arts certificate"... which is a great name for a brand of toilet paper.

It became immediately clear that college, even "drama school," was not a natural fit for me. Having hidden away those four years of high school, I was not used to being told what to do and basically allergic to being around people my own age. My grotesque commitment to trying to feel like the most interesting person in every room I entered was a lot harder to manage at a place like the University of North Carolina School of the Arts. No one warned me that drama schools were essentially a snake pit of people with the same egotistical need to feel special that I had. When everyone is desperate to be celebrated, it's hard for any celebration to ever get going at all.

I immediately hit it off with a fellow classmate, Joshua Morgan, who rivaled me in his level of show queenliness, and I quickly started avoiding schoolwork to instead focus on writing musicals with him. Josh was good at balancing both the actual reason we were taking out student loans and writing together during our downtime. But I couldn't get comfortable just agreeing to go along with the tedious process of higher education and following rules.

Within my first few months, I'd already gotten into trouble for writing a pretty unkind musical about our dance teacher and staging readings in empty rehearsal rooms in the middle of the night. The teacher had been a chorus girl in a flop Mary Martin musical called *Jennie*, and that just wasn't something I could let go of. When I think back on that time, all those unlocked rehearsal rooms, and all the gorgeous nineteen-year-old dancers I could've been having sex with instead of lampooning my teacher through subpar musical comedy, I have to try really hard not to cry over all those wasted ballet butts.

There was no real reason for my eventual running away from school: no humiliating experience performing a scene from *All My Sons* in class; no tap combination from *Stop the World: I Want to Get Off* that I just couldn't crack. It was as simple as the fact that I wanted to go back to hiding. So I did what I always did: I stopped my world so I could get off. By that point, running away felt as routine as putting on pants one leg at a time or masturbating while watching the locker room scene in *The Best Little Whorehouse in Texas* . . . it's just what you do.

Despite the fact that Joshua and I were extremely close—we'd even gotten the school to switch our housing so we could be roommates—I didn't tell him I was leaving. That would have required some form of accountability, and I think we can all agree that accountability wasn't slithering around my particular can of worms. Instead, I packed up my bedroom in the middle of the night, making an effort to do so as quietly as possible so I didn't wake anyone up. Then I waited until Joshua and my other roommates left to go to class for the day before making my escape. Just as I hit the final stop sign before pulling off campus into my reckless freedom and hiding, Joshua came walking up the sidewalk on his way back to the apartment to pick up something he'd forgotten. He stopped, staring quizzically at me and my car, which was loaded full of stuff like I was Jed Clampett leaving Silver Dollar City in the opening credits of *The Beverly Hillbillies*.

"Jeffery? Where are you going with all your stuff?" he asked, a mix of surprise and disappointment in knowing exactly what I was doing.

"I can't," I said, caught red-handed and with a lump in my throat. I was horrified at this forced moment of goodbye, the type of moment I'd perfected avoiding with eighteen years of speed racing away. "I just can't," I added as I pulled the car ahead and drove through the school gates onto the main road, braving a glimpse back at Joshua watching me go.

It was an exhilarating feeling, driving out of Winston-Salem and knowing that no one besides Joshua knew I had just run away from college, and no one even knew where I was. I was running and hiding all at once. While I had mentioned wanting to leave to Tanya, the teacher I mentioned earlier, I knew she wouldn't tell a soul. I gripped the steering wheel to stop my nerves from trembling, choosing instead to shake along to the original cast recording of *Hairspray*. Perhaps my body knew I was making a mistake, perhaps I was afraid of getting in trouble, perhaps I was just excited to run and hide, or perhaps I shook because, as Marc Shaiman and Scott Wittman's *Hairspray* lyrics attest, "You can't stop the beat." No matter what, I knew I was excited, the type of excitement you only get from running away. When you run and hide, there's always something next. There's always somewhere to run to. There's always the teeny tiny chance that you are going to feel better wherever you end up hiding next.

About an hour into my journey, my phone rang. It was Robert, the assistant dean of the drama school. He was a very kind man whom I had immediately bonded with from day one, by which

I mean he was a totally flaming dandy who had graduated from Juilliard with Christine Baranski and who treated me like a king. When I glanced down at the incoming call, I knew I'd been found out. My first instinct was to be pissed off at Joshua for ratting me out, and my second was that I—oh fuck!—needed to tell my parents what I'd done. I had, of course, not mentioned to either of them that I was even considering dropping out of the college they had cosigned copious student loans to pay for, let alone that I was going to do so the week before spring break. Or that I was currently driving to their house at that very moment.

Sweating and panicked, I pulled over onto the side of the freeway. Two months earlier, I'd totaled a car on that very road while changing a David Sedaris audio book CD in the midst of rush hour traffic and a torrential downpour. I listened to Robert's voicemail; he begged me to call him and insisted that I simply turn the car around and come back to school. He was clearly distraught and hurt on a personal level, acknowledging that he thought I trusted him after I had made him the first call two months earlier when I'd hydroplaned off the freeway and totaled my car. Robert had been more than an assistant dean to me; he had been my friend. It was Robert who sent two fellow students to pick me up from the rest stop where I waited with a very nice police officer after my car accident. It was Robert who had championed my getting a campus theater to produce the cabaret show I'd directed my class in a month earlier. It was Robert who'd gotten tears in his eyes telling me about the time he'd met Katharine Hepburn in the window of her limo after seeing her in a matinee of *Coco*, the only musical she ever did (thank God). But I hadn't told Robert anything about wanting to leave, and I certainly wasn't going to call him back and open my heart now that I had. Once you start running you don't stop. I hit IGNORE before calling my parents and confessing that I'd dropped out of college.

"I'll be home in four hours, depending on traffic," I said, emotionless because there were too many to choose from.

"And then what?" my infuriated dad asked.

I paused and shrugged, which you can't hear on a phone, before hanging up and continuing to drive. I had no fucking clue. Hide, I reckoned.

The months that followed were a pretty bleak premonition of the pitch-black lows that would become a second language to my psyche in the years to come. I went back to my homeschool routine but now without the sham of "schoolwork" looming over my head. Meanwhile, all my classmates at drama school were moving on from silent Stanislavsky acting exercises to real scene work from classic plays. I couldn't help but wake up every day, stare at my childhood bedroom ceiling, and think, *Oh boy, now you've really done it*. Instead of mending my error of running, maybe even begging the school to take me back, I unfriended all my classmates on Facebook.

Life quickly had a *Groundhog Day* quality. I had tasted something that resembled dreams coming true only to run away from it and back into the monotony of whatever the purgatory is that exists between being a teenager and finally growing up.

It wasn't long before I became infatuated with a guy going to the Bible college across the street from my parents, and I did all sorts of nutty, codependent things in the process. With nothing else to do, I joined his social life with theater majors who were impressed enough by me because I'd lived in New York that I felt comfortable getting blackout drunk with them every weekend. The guy ended up being the first person I ever had full-blown sex with, but true to form, I eventually made a complete fool of myself and ran away from his circle entirely.

After a few months of this, I realized I had to either get out of my hometown and back to New York or develop a crystal meth addiction to speed up my self-destruction. I'd heard meth could give you acne and rot your teeth, so I set my sights back on New York instead. That summer, Joshua, the friend from school, offered an olive branch to the friendship I'd run away from. He invited me to join him in his New Jersey hometown to direct a reading of a really, really bad musical we had written the year prior. I did so, traveling in a pair of flip-flops and carrying a backpack with three pairs of underwear, a couple of T-shirts, and yet another collection of plays. It was like those old-school great escapes to the tree across the street, except back then I would make a big deal about saying goodbye. Now, even though I knew I was never coming back, I told my family I'd see them in a few weeks.

Surprising no one—except my parents somehow—I didn't return home. Instead, I kept kicking my return further and further down the road until the road disappeared entirely. My mom would call me in tears, explaining that this wasn't the agreement, that I was supposed to have come back, that she knew I would eventually move away but that I owed her a goodbye before doing so. "You don't even have shoes!" she would cry into the phone before I'd mercilessly hang up on her.

This was not the way to get me back. In fact, the minute she proposed the idea of me coming back to properly pack up my life and say my goodbyes before taking my next steps forward, it became the absolute last thing I was ever going to do. Instead, I forced my way back into the friend's apartment I'd stayed in during my time working as a director's assistant and slowly put together the next chapter. This included working in the gift shop at New York City Opera before becoming a full-time sex worker . . . from gay to gayer. The following period in New York, between ages eighteen and twenty-three, was full of more running and hiding. That's the great thing about a city as populous as New York: you don't have to go far to run and reinvent. Throughout the next five years, I ran from one friendship group to another to another until I eventually ran away from New York altogether.

It happened after the second season of *Jeffery and Cole Casserole*. Cole and I were performing a monthly variety show at Joe's Pub. This show always consisted of us doing a reading of a play we'd written, along with guest variety performances. While we had built our previous shows to be highly scripted sketches that never put me on the spot, this was more freewheeling and spontaneous, and I was beyond out of my depth. A combination of sex work fatigue, constant financial woes, and the constant comparing myself to Cole had created a perfect storm of indulgent diffidence.

The last performance we ever did together featured Bridget Everett and Erin Markey (dressed as Big Bird) doing their musical acts before Cole and I performed individually. Bridget and Erin are two of the most talented performers of all time, and they killed, as did Cole. They all sang songs and produced classic variety show magic. I, however, chose to read a sappy personal essay about when a Disney TV movie was filmed outside my grandparents' house in the early nineties. When you attempt to do something that tedious following Bridget Everett belting "Colors of the Wind" while sitting on people's faces, you're going to fail. Of course, I didn't realize that until I read the pretentious and ultimately dull story to the type of bored silence meant for "a moment of" following a national tragedy.

Once the show ended, I was such a wreck that I didn't even come onstage to bow. Instead, I locked myself in a bathroom stall and cried, as usual. After I rallied myself out of the bathroom, I beelined it out of Joe's Pub, where a random audience member was waiting to get a photo with Bridget. He was a bitchy drunk at a cabaret show, but the minute he engaged with me, I handed him all possible power over my emotions. I knew I'd failed. Now all I needed was someone to rub salt in the wounds, and luckily for me I didn't have to look far.

I can't remember exactly what he said, but I imagine it was something along the lines of praising all the other performers, then pointing out the silence that had followed my oddly chosen "personal essay." With an aloof shrug, he put the final nail in the coffin of a horrible night.

So, naturally, I burst into tears and stormed all the way uptown to my apartment in Hell's Kitchen, skipping out on the after-party everyone else was going to, and hid in my bed for twenty-four hours.

The next day, I ran again. I'd had plans to go visit LA and I'd found someone to sublet my room for the two weeks I'd be gone, and as I packed up my little duffel, I looked around my bedroom of stuff and knew I would never set foot in that room again.

I saw Cole before I left. I don't remember what we did, but I do remember saying goodbye on a subway platform. I knew I was leaving New York for good, and all things Jeffery and Cole along with it. Of course, I didn't say any of that. I simply said my usual, "I'll see you in a couple weeks!"

Two weeks turned into a month, and eventually I called my roommates to say I wasn't coming back and that they could have everything in my room or throw it out. The person I'd found to sublet took over my bedroom, and my kind roommates were forced into having a new tenant. Finally, I told Cole I was staying in LA, and while they were somewhat shocked, I think they also knew it was time for them to do something else as well. I ran away, and this time the place I ran to hide was sunny and sparklingly new. I was staying in my friend Guy Branum's centrally located West Hollywood apartment, and a new chapter began despite the fact that I'd once again run away from the previous one without any sort of conclusion.

As tends to happen in LA, I blinked and a lot of time passed. Thirteen years. I had plenty of life in that time. There was the grade A shitstorm of my relationship and then breakup with my first boyfriend, which culminated in that pesky restraining order. There were two books that I wrote way too quickly in a rush and from an uninspired place, books that I now would pay good money to make disappear. These were followed by two young adult books I don't hate. There was a seemingly endless cycle of rejections following TV show pitches, auditions, first dates, and messy hookups.

There was a lot of joy too. I made incredible friends with whom I spent many wonderful days making creative projects and even better nights celebrating them. There were a handful of TV pilots I got paid good money to be in but that weren't picked up and that no one ever saw. One of them even gave me three dreamy weeks filming on location in Atlanta with not just the great Andie MacDowell but also Kathleen fucking Turner. I quickly made it my mission to be their best friend on set, accomplishing it and further broadening a not-so-friendly gap between them in the process. The pilot itself wasn't very good, but on my darkest days I can always remind myself that not only did I once take Rachel Bilson (she was the lead) to a male strip club in Atlanta where you could smoke inside (Rachel left faster than you could say "emphysema") but that I also, more than once, smoked American Spirits (the blue box kind) while drinking airplane-size bottles of vodka from the hotel minibar in Kathleen Turner's room as the sun flooded the garden of the Atlanta Ritz-Carlton after a week of night shoots. If that's not joy, then I simply don't know what is.

Most of all, though, I discovered that LA is the absolute best place to hide. You can exist in LA without ever really having to engage in the world beyond development deals and being "pinned for availability" to be in a pilot for a role that will undoubtedly go to someone younger, hotter, and straighter. In all those years in LA, I never ran, but I got very, very good at hiding.

You'd think it'd be the opposite in Southern California, with the multitude of freeways, nearby diverse climates, friendly cults . . . that the impulse to run would be at its greatest. But for me, the slow pace permitted me to choose the opposite: to settle into an unchallenged routine of weed smoking, movie watching, talking about writing yet rarely doing it, and—ugh, sure—hiking.

When I was filming the show *Search Party*, the main perk (aside from employment and working with one of my best friends, Charles Rogers) was that I was flown to New York once a year and put up in a furnished apartment for months at a time. This sufficiently scratched my itch to return to New York until the show ended and I realized that I didn't want to fill the rest of my days getting stoned and wandering around various Southern California Target stores . . . which, if I'm being honest, was practically my full-time job. Not working at them. Just wandering around them.

I tried to convince myself that hiding the rest of my days in mine and Augie's house in East LA was the answer to all my problems, insecurities, and fears. I tried to embrace the idea that I would eventually be one of those quirky *Day of the Locust*–type people you meet in dimly lit Hollywood bars, brimming over with amusing stories and a murky connection to something resembling a career. The type of person who briefly captures your attention as he tells you, through red wine breath so hot you could warm your hands on it, about the two scenes he did with Betty White on *Hot in Cleveland* in 2010. (I had the flu the day we filmed and was 80 percent sure I was contagious enough to kill her but comforted myself with the reminder that it would make a great story for a book like this someday.) There's something quietly glamorous about those Nathanael West–type So-Cal barflies, and over the years I'd almost convinced myself that slowly becoming one could feel whatever comes between obsolete and complacent.

But I couldn't stop the nagging feeling in my soul that it was time to pack up and change before I gradually sank into the La Brea Tar Pits next to the woolly mammoths, the Black Dahlia, and all of the failed pilots Shelley Long did after *Cheers*.

However, I was equally terrified by the notion of running back to the slipstream of unfinished business I'd left behind in New York. When you run away, it's harder to come back and pretend things are normal. I suppose that's the whole point of running in the first place.

It was in the midst of filming a "gay bitch in a scarf"–type guest star role on an episode of *iCarly* for Paramount Plus (please, this isn't the time to ask for autographs!) that whatever was holding me back from setting fire to my current easy life in LA vanished, and I could do nothing else but dream of running back to New York.

We sold our house, our cars, and a lot of our belongings and made the move back to New York City. The difference with this move was that, for the very first time, moving didn't equal running. Instead, I was forced to experience the arduously uncomfortable process of packing up our lives, tying up loose ends, saying goodbye to beloved friends, properly closing the door to one chapter, and intentionally opening the door to the next. It was scary, complicated, heavy, unpredictable, and icky. Just as the best of life and bespoke cheeses usually are.

I had never left a place without leaving behind some unresolved chaos in my wake, breaking the Swiffer before having to swiff up my mess. I felt the same sad tug at my heart as when I bid farewell to that visiting theater company in my hometown. The same fear of what's next as when I left New York at seventeen after realizing I wasn't quite ready for that much life yet. The same fear of being hated, but the same hope that this time things would be better than every previous moment of running. But instead of hiding in a bathroom or running into the woods, I watched the movers put all our stuff in a van, and we waved goodbye, telling all our belongings we'd see them on the other side of the country.

Upon returning to New York, we moved into a lovely apartment in the West Village on one of those cobblestone streets that feel haunted by both turn-of-the-century ghosts and Sarah Jessica Parker. In fact, when we were turning the corner to visit the building for the first time, we came face-to-face with none other than the mayor of Lower Manhattan herself, looking so quintessentially SJP with her effortlessly chic Sunday attire and Three Lives bookstore tote bag that it couldn't have been more New York if I'd found myself in line at Russ & Daughters behind the Statue of Liberty herself. For a person who believes in signs, this felt as obvious a good one as any.

It was an ecstatic feeling of joy to be back in the type of city where one out of ten people know who Donna Murphy is. Of course, once we had finished the business of setting up our apartment and getting into the groove of our new lives, the ever-familiar voices of self-doubt and shame began their never-ending mental cabaret show with a two-drink minimum. Once you slow down from running and start walking for the first time, it's more than a little disorienting. Like Serena Williams playing badminton. When you're used to it, running and hiding is quite simply easier than any alternative. If the road is paved and you do it correctly, you don't even have to wear shoes.

But now here I am, finishing this book in my new apartment in the West Village, the haunted cobblestone street outside, and Sarah Jessica Parker mere blocks away—in the words of Norma Desmond, somewhere out there in the dark. It would be certifiably insane not to feel inspired in such conditions and even crazier not to be at least adjacent to happy. But of course, if you've made it this far, you know that I am more than very capable of crazy things. Because underneath any sort of hopeful resolution or aha moment, I know that, along with the magic of SJP sightings on cobblestone streets, also lurks the worst of my mind and moods. All the worst parts of myself: the too big a sense of self, the too small a sense of self, creating content for myself that absolutely no one else wants, self-doubt, self-hate, self-harm, selfishness, self-centeredness, self-absorption, self-pity, clearly a lot of self-obsession, and . . . let me set the scene to finish this list:

We're now at that annoyingly awkward moment in the already not so great play you've gone to see at Manhattan Theatre Club starring the brilliant Laura Linney. Her character is doing some sort of busywork that characters in a play do but that no one does in real life, like polishing silver with toothpaste and paper towels. The audience's fidgeting to go the fuck home briefly stops as Laura Linney puts a glistening salad spoon down onto a reflective sterling silver bowl in the fully realized kitchen set built by an award-winning scenic designer. She looks up at the painstakingly designed-for-this-moment pin spot gelled in "bastard amber" and as casually as a person can while stating the title of something a room of eight hundred people have already purchased a ticket to . . . in a projected, yet trembling, voice with the light perfectly hitting the intricate cheekbones of her beautiful face . . . Laura Linney looks past the back row to an exit sign as she casually drolls to no one but us in particular: "Self-sabotage."

So yeah, as I predicted pages and pages, hours and hours, drafts and drafts, and many emotional highs and lows ago . . . this has been a sort of note to self. A reminder that while, yes, life can sometimes suck and things can go the opposite of planned, the only way forward is to breathe and wait before I burn it all down, to think before I sabotage my life. There is plenty of joy, plenty of inspiration, and plenty of tomorrow left. But only if I get the fuck out of my own way . . . and out of bed while I'm at it.

Somehow, despite my never-ending impulse to the contrary, I have yet to even sabotage this very book. My inner demons have certainly done all their deeply on-brand things to try but I have somehow yet to throw my laptop into the fire while finishing these stories. I have yet to email my publishers to say, "Forget it." I have yet to let my breakdowns stop my deadlines. I have yet to try and cancel myself by taking to the cesspool known as Instagram to post a (perfectly okay) picture of myself dressed as Whoopi Goldberg in 2011 that I recently spent months trying to scrub from the internet. No, there was no offensive makeup, but yes, there was a regrettable dreadlock wig and, if I do say so myself, a perfect costume of the type of comfortably fabulous clothing my number one queen Whoopi wears every morning at ten on *The View* (check your local listings).

I truly have no clue what happens next, and while writing this book I was reminded of just how far away I've grown from the confidence, ambition, and perseverance I had once upon a time; it feels like so long ago, but maybe it was just yesterday or the day before that. My always evolving and devolving existence—as a writer, an actor, and whatever the hell else I find myself being labeled for a paycheck—continues to shift from success to failure in a tango that never seems to stop. I still haven't achieved the bulk of my dreams and often suspect that a lot of them are simply not meant to be. However, I am attempting to convince myself that the mere fact that you're currently holding this book, or listening to it, or having someone else hold it for you if you're super rich and lazy (good for you!) is some indication that the hateful music in my head is simply that: in my head.

I am hoping this book represents a promise to myself to see the next page in my life as a fresh start without the guilt of a trash heap I have left behind. As I've been forced to step back and look at so much of the mess I've made in the past almost forty years, the mountain of shame I've found myself running and hiding from time and time again doesn't look nearly as tall and menacing as it did before I started writing all of it down.

I attempt to promise myself that I will stay on course, keep moving ahead, but not try and make it a race. Sure, there will be uncomfortable goodbyes, jobs I don't get, dreams that don't come true, broken hearts, things I'm not good at it, people more talented and successful than me, days and nights I will wonder if I'm capable of getting through, and people who really dislike me. Maybe even abominable backstage moms with ugly haircuts or booing cruise ship audiences that would much prefer Charo to me (join the club, pal!). But no matter where the next part of my story twists and turns, it's a path worth committing to because it's the very path that's led me here. And ultimately, when you stop running, when you catch your breath and come out of your hiding spot in the woods with your bag of snacks and a volume of Neil Simon plays, with whatever you were hiding from now behind you, you look around and realize that here isn't so bad after all.

# Acknowledgments

This book wouldn't have been possible without my absolutely fantastic editor, Rakesh Satyal, who saw something in my stories and nurtured them every step of the way with kindness and encouragement. My thanks go out to him and the rest of HarperOne, especially assistant editor Ryan Amato. I'd also like to thank my agent, Alex Kane, and my lawyers, Seth Horowitz and David Berlin. Along with the brilliant friends who read pages as I wrote them and offered helpful thoughts and constant support: Cole Escola, Jacob Wasson, Gideon Glick, Ben Rimalower, and Charles Rogers. Thank you to my beautiful husband, Augie Prew, for not only putting up with me on a daily basis but also listening to me read each word of this book aloud through years of rewrites and always offering new ideas and love. And finally, just as I finished the copy edit process of this book my dear friend Eric Gilliland passed away. I thank him for nearly two decades of enormous support.

# About the Author

Jeffery Self is a writer and actor whose TV credits include *Search Party*, *The Horror of Dolores Roach*, *Shameless*, *30 Rock*, and *Desperate Housewives*, as well as cocreating and starring in the cult lo-fi series *Jeffery & Cole Casserole* with Cole Escola. His film credits include *Drop*, *Spoiler Alert*, *Mack and Rita*, and *The High Note*. He is the author of the young adult novels *Drag Teen* and *A Very, Very Bad Thing*. He lives in New York City.